24 Directions at Once

Dispatches from the COVID-19 Lockdown

By Jim Blackwood, Jr.

No Clock Books

Portland, Oregon 97215

www.jimblackwoodjr.com

First Edition

ISBN: 978-1-7355599-0-2

ISBN: 978-1-7355599-1-9 (ebook)

DEDICATION

FOR EVERYONE who gave of themselves so that others may live during our pandemic. Especially our essential workers who made the ultimate sacrifice.

Be Smart. Be Compassionate. Wash those hands. Wear your mask!

Also by Jim Blackwood:

*Am I Cured Yet? My Wonderful Life
with Panic Disorder and PTSD*

THE ESSAYIST is a self-liberated man, sustained by the childish belief that everything he thinks about, everything that happens to him, is of general interest. He is a fellow who thoroughly enjoys his work, just as people who take bird walks enjoy theirs. Each new excursion of the essayist, each new 'attempt,' differs from the last and takes him into new country. This delights him. Only a person who is congenitally self-centered has the effrontery and stamina to write essays.

~ E.B. White, 1977

CONTENTS

UNPREDICTABLE

———————————

WHO AMONG US had 'pandemic' marked on our calendars? Not me. It's the world-wide storm that demands our attention. Some things unify us: life, death, children, dogs, cats, the smell of the air after a hard rain. Now, humanity is sharing something enormous. We are all living chapters of the same horrific, scary book. Life has been altered and the always present uncertainty has reconfigured itself as a piercing siren and universal blinking light. We don't like what is happening to us because tamping down uncertainty is our life's work. If we are limber, with feet planted firmly on the ground, we bend and sway like a willow tree in a storm. When the battering wind passes, there we are, fully upright again … well, not always.

This confusing time inspired me to embrace the randomness of my life in this collection of essays. Try though I might, I could not rope these works into neat, logical corrals. Some mornings when we wake up, we have a plan, a bold direction. Then, with the first news, a call, a text, an email, an ache, a sniffle or a quiet conversation with a stranger, off we go in another direction, unknown and uncharted. When I realized how automatically we stumble into this fate, I let go of the need to organize these essays. They come as life does, one thing after the other, both chaotic and utterly predictable.

This collection began as an escape plan from a memoir I spent over a year writing, editing, and publishing. I was happy with how I told my story but to my shock I discovered that even a big fat memoir becomes a prison of sorts. To tell a coherent, and hopefully engaging, story I had resisted my ever-present temptation to roam off into the distance on delicious tangents. I mostly succeeded but those thought expeditions were still alive and kicking. With no little irony, a plague gave these new tales the time they needed to come to life. Never waste a pandemic.

Each essay is a meditation on a single word. I will leave it to you to discover when the essay begat the word or the word inspired the essay. This collection is not the detritus gathered from the cutting room floor of my first book. I didn't attempt to tell a previous story better. I did mine random notes I had scribbled for months in the margins of previous draft manuscripts. I was most interested in what I chose not to say and why. Sometimes the negative space is the essential point of the painting.

There is a bedrock of two cities under this book. I grew up in Indio, California, a place that in my childhood was a relatively isolated, blue collar town in the Southern California desert. Like many of us desert rats, I never completely shook the sand out of my boots. The other place is Portland, Oregon, my home for over three decades. It is a city of rivers, bridges, and trees. On the color wheel, the two places are brown, then green. These bookended homes could not be more different. But if we are lucky, the places we live become characters in our lives.

The thread that binds these essays is that they were written during our great pandemic amidst the strange time of on-again, off-again, on-again confinement. I love this writing work but lacking the ability to move about freely, this collection became both a welcome friend and the annoying, overstay-the-welcome house guest.

For months, I held out a reward for my efforts—a celebratory trip from my little home office with its lockdown winter to spring to summer view of our back porch. For reasons that now seem fanciful, I kept the hope that each new week would mean our release. I had a plan. Once I had a first draft manuscript printed, three-hole punched and neatly loaded into my favorite blue, three-ring binder, I would walk to my closest (one of the bazillions in Portland) coffee shop, order a large latte and something sweet, curled and cinnamon. I would then camp out at a table near one of the street view windows and merrily scrawl through the pages with my trusty hard lead-filled mechanical pencil. For months, I played this little scene at night as my head hit the pillow, a bedtime story.

Well, you can guess the rest. I gave up and ordered a cheap coffee maker from our omnipresent online beast of a store and bought a plastic wrapped sweet roll at the supermarket. Damn this virus. I trust my tiny broken heart did not leak into what follows.

WAITING

EVERYTHING LOOKS THE SAME. The trees. The sky. The streets. The houses. The stores. Color hasn't changed. The greens are still green. The grey skies still feel dreary. The sun is still warm. People move the same. Dogs still bark. Now, if in those first few moments of the day, stirring from my pillow, I could only remember what day it was.

I have read about times past when events had conspired to turn the world on its head. Wars, earthquakes, plagues, tsunamis. Twirling a pencil in my fingers, I wondered how I would behave in such disasters. Would I rise to the occasion, be brave for myself and others? Would events conspire to overwhelm me? How would I prepare for the unknowable? Would I survive? Every world changing crisis I studied required greatness in leadership and steadfastness in the people who endured the disruption to daily life for weeks, months, and years. What I had not anticipated was that my test, a test for the entire world, would mostly be about waiting.

My fascination with the coronavirus began with the earliest reports out of China. I poked around the internet for reports. Central China seemed very far away and what was happening there seemed unique. Millions of people isolated in Wuhan by a military cordon. Hospitals appearing almost overnight. Stories of confusion and courage. And ... the masks. In every report, every picture people were in masks, from a simple face covering to elaborate virus blocking rigs. Where did they get all of those masks so fast?

It is easy to watch a disaster at a distance. Truth be told, at a distance is almost always how most of us experience a disaster. We are all crisis voyeurs. Oh, we text the right numbers to send money, are sad at the stories of individual loss, happy at the stories of courage and persistence, but mostly, if we pay attention at all, another person's crisis is simply how we fill a few minutes a day. I am more than guilty. I love to watch hurricanes come onshore on cable news to see those little funnel maps of where the hurricane may land. I stay up late to heckle the silly reporters who stand in the wind and the rain when they could have just as easily stepped behind the protection of a wall. I watch the aftermath, all that water, boats, and people in hip waders. For a couple of days, I am a hurricane response expert.

Something about watching Wuhan lock down and all those people in masks struck me as different. In early February, well before most people were paying attention, I ordered face masks. I felt a little silly and when they arrived slid them into a drawer thinking they would be a curious artifact. My wife, always the 'big one' earthquake prepper, said that unknown to me, she had put a few masks in our earthquake kit years ago. At least with her, I felt less like an alarmist goofball. We made one last unmasked trip to the grocery store to buy things we never buy: powdered milk, a stack of chicken soup cans, powdered Gatorade, saltine crackers for when the bread disappeared off shelves, and toilet paper. We didn't need the toilet paper but the crowd on that aisle inspired a little panic. Already, for a few in the checkout line, there was a palpable sense of caution. When people are not sure what to do, they still do something. Then the virus did what millions of people do every day; it flew around the world.

I started waiting. I knew it was coming. There was no way to know what that would mean, but I was so convinced this event would be important that on Leap Day, February 29, I started an pandemic blog. (Of course, I did.) That rhyme in old The Knack song, "My Sharona," was stuck in my head so I called it My Corona Log: People Pandemics Politics. Even then, with a sense of irony, I grabbed a dust mask from my toolbox, pulled a black hoodie over my head, cinched the mask to my face, and had my wife take a picture of me in front of my computer. (I couldn't wait to get the mask off as it was so uncomfortable. Ignorance was still bliss.) Now I had a banner page for the new website. I was in a mask. Another silly artifact, I thought, as I made the site live. I would wait with everyone else … on the internet.

Most sane people limit their doses of bad news. It's too upsetting. I become a sponge, taking in all the information I can find in a futile attempt to manage my anxiety with knowledge. People tell me, "Oh, that would depress me." It doesn't bring me down. The more I know the easier it is to become an observer, create a space between me and what is going on around me. The observer then becomes the communicator, as I write my way through things. While most people were still unaware, I was searching the internet for epidemiologists and clinicians. I read papers where I was lucky to understand every fourth sentence. I looked at models. Now everyone looks at models. Like my hurricane expertise, I became the worst sort of dilettante, an internet virus expert. You know those people, right? Yeah, I was that insufferable guy. Still, the actual virus was beyond arm's length. It was somewhere else. But I knew it was coming.

When the quarantine finally came, I was relieved. This was the only way we were going to keep our hospitals from being overrun. For days I had been yelling at my television screen for governors to act fast. When our governor did finally lock us down, I felt like a winner for about five minutes before I thought, "what now?" I had been waiting for the virus to get here, waiting for the government to act, waiting for the states to all lock down. I realized that what I had actually been wishing for was more waiting.

Once I walk out the door of my home, everything I do requires waiting. I wait until I think the lines at the grocery store will be social distanced and shorter. Before I get out of my car, I wait to put on my mask. I reach into my pocket and press the button to open the truck lock, so I don't have touch my keys when I get back to the car. Once in the store, I look down aisles and wait patiently for the other shoppers to clear the space in front of what I need. Every step I take is a calculation of how to maintain my safe distance. The simplest acts now require a slow-motion ballet. Once home, the refrigerated goods have to be cleaned on the back porch. Dry goods wait for a day in the garage. The Cheerios detox cheerlessly.

A walk to the park is almost exactly the same as it ever was, which makes it all the stranger when I see someone in the distance about to meet me at the same street corner. When our individual radars ping each other a new waiting negotiation begins. Who will take the intersection first?

Who will pause or slow down or speed up? Maybe a quick nod. And then, negotiation complete, space defined. As our safety bubbles touch, if we are maskless, we offer flat-mouthed smiles under quick eye connections. When we have masks, then every bit of humanity has to be communicated with the eyes alone. But that's fine. Humans adapt surprisingly fast from reading an entire face to reading the eyes alone. The flat smile muscles move the eyes enough so that we both know what we just did.

Underlying the newly elaborate ballet of the now mind-numbingly repeated cycle of daily life is the big wait. Consciously and unconsciously, we are waiting to get sick. Spring pollen, the scratchy cough of allergies take on a new meaning. Cough. Is this it? What is the quality of that cough? Dry cough? Did I cough like this last allergy season? Hand to face. Am I warm? What was the last time I came into contact with someone or something that may have had the virus? How many days? Four or five? As a nervous person, a practicing hypochondriac, I have always been a highly tuned body monitor. But now, with each possible COVID-19 symptom, I run an overused check list. I am waiting to get sick.

When the waves of illness hit hardest in Italy, I read how people there lived with COVID-19. I wondered how they knew when to go to the hospital. Hospitals now seemed like dangerous places to be avoided until the last, maybe the actual last, minute. Everywhere I looked people talked about oxygen in the blood. Don't let it get below 95 percent. Not completely sure what that meant, I joined millions of people looking on the internet for a pulse oximeter. Herd fear. I finally found one at an inflated price and ordered it. It, too, waits in a drawer. Chicken soup and a pulse oximeter. What a strange crisis.

If I am not waiting to get sick, then I am waiting for those I love to succumb to the illness. Greetings, almost always electronic these days, have subtly moved from to "hello" to "feeling okay?" There is an old Chinese greeting of "have you eaten today?" I wonder if this will go on long enough to change how we greet one another. I actually like the idea of saying hello by asking about someone's health. It seems both more intimate and, well, too intimate.

Our home has become *Upstairs/Downstairs*. Eight years younger, my wife is not retired. A couple of years into my retirement I had built a happy collection of patterns around my passions. Write, think, play with the dogs, baseball in the summer, live music in small clubs, and film study (well … beer, pizza, and a movie) at my favorite non-profit theater. Very rapidly, we had to convert our upstairs space into a home office for my wife. We retire to our levels during the day, meeting in the kitchen for coffee or lunch. The two dogs divide their loyalties up and down the stairs based on mysterious factors that only clarify with the crinkle of a potato chip bag. Of all my happiest out-of-home diversions, only gardening still exists.

My wife's work hours have been reduced and we both wait to see if her job survives. This means that, like millions of Americans, we are waiting to see what our financial future becomes. We have worked hard and have some means. Many in the grip of the COVID-19 economic meltdown are far worse off. I think about my barber and my favorite bartender. We used to give money to a collection of good causes. Now Sally and I divert our gifts to food banks and small businesses we love. There is some satisfaction in that effort. However, while we wait for financial clarity, too many people are waiting to see when they will once again have a job, a business, a place to live, a bag of groceries to survive another week. We will have to figure out the virus before we restore the economy. I wonder, are we now waiting for another Great Depression?

In my international disaster playbook was the emergence of a great, unifying national leader. As if there was a cosmic waiting room filled with the right people, I was thinking that folks like Churchill or Roosevelt or Lincoln were always going to show up right when we needed them. Those are leaders who faced years long crises and found a way to motivate their populations by neatly layering hope and fear in a way that engendered a spirit of 'we are all in this together.' If any situation was ready-made for such a leader, it is COVID-19. The pandemic knows no ethnicity or philosophical boundaries. In its relentless spread, this is the great egalitarian crisis. Boy, was I wrong. This one was a gimme and yet here we are still waiting for a national plan and ... what's that called ... a president.

I suppose in a world where everything is outsourced from dinner to your Uber ride to see Aunt Jean, I should have known that this president would outsource responding to a pandemic to fifty governors with disparate understandings of their role and completely different constituencies. Of course, that makes perfect sense. I remember a time when in order to go in and out of California every car was stopped at the border for the ominous question, "Are you carrying fruits or vegetables?" Stutter when saying "no" and you got the finger, the point to the canopy where the car was dismantled looking for a scary contraband orange or apple. The border agents were looking for bugs. Now at national borders and state lines we recreate the border bug hunts. To move about the country and the world, now we wait.

On a daily basis, unless you are Woody Allen, it is possible to not think about death. If you are more religious, you get to visit death more regularly as one of the big reasons to have religion at all. Of course, everyone gets to know the death of others and grieve. But think about it; beyond those times, we get off pretty easy. We get large blocks of time where we don't even think about our demise. It's kind of nice. Well … not anymore. There on the right of almost every cable channel screen are two counters. At the top we have the 'Damn, that's a huge number of sick people' tally and below we see dead people. Most alarming is that between the morning shows and the nightly news both counters are spinning up. So now, turn on the news and you get a relentless reminder that the most fundamental human problem underlies the pandemic. We are waiting to die. And, to double down on the terror, we now all know that once sick, we die alone. No family. No friends. Overworked strangers, each one living in peril, in masks, who hope you are not their future, too. Oh, and those funeral plans, all neatly written down or told with solemnity to family; forget about it. Body out the door to the freezer trailer and maybe a Zoom grief session. But those, too, will have to wait until everyone can get connected to the internet.

Some of us are going to be waiting for a long time. I am a guy in his 60s with a family history of heart disease. In fact, about seventy million people in America are over 60, in the cohort of folks for whom COVID-19 is exceedingly dangerous. Those immortal young people are learning lessons, too. Anxious to party as things reopened, they went too far and now line up for ICU beds. The virus doesn't count birthdays. It doesn't care if you are bored. But for us older folks to return to slices of normal we wait for a vaccine. Old enough to recall how a sugar cube once cured polio, we are relegated to the role of observers. Every day we will look at what used to be the mindless actions of life and ask ourselves, "Is it safe?" And, as a guy whose greatest joys were settling into a seat with popcorn at a movie and pressing up front to get a closer look at the band at a club show, I can't begin to think when I will be at either of those places once more. I have no choice but to wait.

All this waiting is not the crisis I had planned on. It feels like a growing series of incomplete acts. Spring without a beer at a game. Friday at the movies without the actual movie theater. A cocktail and dinner with friends without the friends. If we do nothing as well as we possibly can, the reward is that nothing happens. Oh, like many, I try to take solace that it's the waiting that saves other people's lives. I am willing to outwait many people. Most of the things I miss the most are things I can actually live without. Too many people have had their waiting ended with a zipped-up body bag. There are doctors and nurses who wait for a moment away from the beeping life support machines. For a guy notorious for his impatience, learning to wait isn't such an awful thing. But truth be told, I can't wait for this to be over.

OPEN

It only took days before I knew
he would always come to find me.

I HAVE NEVER BEEN COMPLETELY SURE what it feels like to be loved. I can't locate that feeling or a sensation. When I see other people showing that they know they are loved, I watch them closely, looking for a clue about what they are actually feeling. Is there a sensation in the chest? The gut? Do they feel it in the arms or do their legs get all wobbly? Does it wash across their faces like a cool breeze? I can't see it. For me, it is a futile exercise.

I have seen that when someone has a child the two-way love is overwhelming and immediate. I don't have kids. I don't know. Oh, to be certain, I feel warmth in the presence of my wife. I feel sad when she is sad and happy when I see her light up with delight. I feel anger when she is abused, and her touch helps me feel calm. Is that what feeling love is like? Is it the assembly of all the emotional component parts? Somehow, that doesn't seem right. For me, those pieces don't become a collective. They surround a certain hollowness inside me. Like a circular house with doors facing in all directions, my core only lets one door open at time. Something about too much openness is frightening.

Every time he greets me is like the first time.

My wife tells me I come from a long line of men who express their love by what they do. That is probably so. If I pull my wife's car into the driveway, clean it, wash and wax it, there is a moment where she comes out to admire my work. I hang on her reaction. I think she first saw my mother do this little interpersonal transaction with my father. The unsolicited effort followed by the acknowledgement of the act. Infinitely more skilled at relationships, my wife saw that this was how the men in my family express our love. We fix things, change things, gather things, and present things. We protect and encourage. To be certain, I am capable of schmaltzy romance and can weave a picture with words to express my adoration, but more commonly I do something seemingly unrelated to relationship that my wife knows is the purest expression of how I feel. It's caretaking as love.

This inability to find a consistent internal location for love may have a corollary. If I can't find it, then no one else can either. Stealth, being elusive, may be the simplest way to protect something that is valuable. I am an expert at concealing my vulnerabilities. I had to be to live with panic disorder. Most people find mental health issues off-putting, so I hid them.

Four generations had come and gone but he was different.

I sometimes wonder if what I call love has been

somehow damaged. Or is everyone's version of love damaged in some way? It is almost impossible to live a long life without giving and receiving it. Because life itself is terminal, even the most lasting expressions of love inevitably end in sadness. It's not a bug, it's a feature. But even in the glorious thrall of being in love, I have felt like I was keeping a secret. Amidst the rushing heart, flushed face … deep within the sweaty, writhing haze of lovemaking … in the quiet release of watching a lover sleep … there was a blank space in the middle of my heart. A safe place I could not reveal. A black hole sucking up the potentially dangerous parts of unbound love.

It is possible to waltz through life and convince oneself you are experiencing the full range of emotions in spite of yourself. Laugh until you cry. Cry until you laugh. Embrace and mourn. Run toward and walk away. If self-awareness includes knowing there is something missing, something protected, something withheld, then I have always been self-aware. What I could not have known was that it wouldn't be a person who would pierce the void. No, that one caught me by surprise.

I had to break eye contact with him before he would do it.

He was a mess when we met. They told us he was a stray only recently caught. Mostly black, with white tips at all the edges: paws, tail, nose, he looked like a fired arrow as he ran in the pen chasing a tennis ball. His emaciated body was an illusion. From the side, he seemed a full-sized dog, but running toward me he was all wrong. Not yet a year old, his frame was built for more than forty pounds. He barely weighed thirty. About a quarter of him was missing. Then there was his coat, so smooth and slick it felt more like human skin. Mostly a Whippet and Border Collie, he could never have much fat on those bones, and he would always need his own pullover jacket on a cold day. I didn't have to think about it twice. We rescued him and called him Zoom, not for his obvious speed, but named after the lead guitar player of the punk band X, Billy Zoom.

My wife and I have a thing for damaged dogs. Some of our new family members took years of careful, slow work to rediscover their place in the world. Zoom taught me about what it was like to be a stray, alone and fending for oneself. To restore him, we needed to give him an astounding 5,000 calories a day. But he was exceedingly cautious about what he would eat. He stalked his food bowl, sniffed and backed away from even the best, most dog yummy treats offered by hand. It was clear that he had had to experiment with found food and sometimes what he ate hurt him.

Even eight years on, he has only begun to sample anything that he can't immediately identify as safe protein. Most strangely, his road dog survival instinct still means he will spit out an egg white but gobble up the yoke. That one baffles me. After a few failed experiments, we found a combination of foods he told us he trusted by finishing the bowl without hesitation. Even then, he purses his lips and uses his front teeth to carefully extract one tiny piece of kibble at a time and drop them around the perimeter of the bowl for close examination. I have no idea how he decides when his food sorting is done but finally, he daintily keeps his nose in the bowl until he is done and then, one by one, slowly eats each of his previous samples from the floor.

Every time I see him bound down the stairs two at a time,
I smile.

After we brought him home, I took several days off

work to help Zoom figure out his new world. We live in an old house with steps to get in and out, stairs to the basement, stairs to our upstairs bedroom. It was instantly apparent that there were no stairs in Zoom's former street world. Stairs terrified him. I don't think he had ever seen them before. At first, I had to lift him up and down the three steps to get to the back yard and back in the house. At the end of the first day, he cautiously navigated that challenge. But nothing would get him up a full staircase. He and his rescue sister, Mozy, would need to spend their days in our basement when we went to work, and his night bed was at the foot of our bed upstairs. Snacks, a happy squeaky toy, feigned excitement, Zen calm. He wasn't having it. I kind of get it. Try getting on your hands and knees and going down some stairs. You quickly discover that it is scary to have your face so far ahead of your body facing down. So first we had to conquer up.

I had to become his body. His will. Not simply drag him up the stairs. I had to live his fear with all the flailing and terror whining. Between my legs, I gently lifted him, first front legs, then back, on step at a time. I couldn't let him do what every impulse in him wanted, to back away and run. While I couldn't absorb any of his fear, he needed to see, feel, that I was not afraid to go up. Now he was shaking, and for me, that was the hardest part. I understood the stubborn resistance that fear creates, but the shaking meant he was giving up, overwhelmed. I knew that state well, but I looked him the in the eyes and softly told him, "You can do this. It's okay. It's okay." Then we were on top. I let go of him and rubbed him down hard all over his body. I wanted to give him a new body sensation. I bathed him with affection and joy.

He then did that thing an animal can do that I always

wished I could do for myself. He shook so hard that he lifted himself off the ground. Trauma released, he once again locked onto my eyes. Then it was down, me in front this time so he looked up at my face. Step by step, no shaking this time, only resistance. Once down, another good shake and we did it again and again until I left him at the bottom of the stairs and called to him from above. He circled and whined, one paw on the first step, then back. "It's okay, Zoom. You can do it." Already responding to his new name, he looked at me now sitting at the top and then he ran up the stairs, flew into my arms.

His most powerful instinct is to seek warmth.

In less than thirty minutes, he figured out how to catch a frisbee in the air and bring it back to me. His two gene pools demanded he chase and catch things. I am a sucker for herding dogs, their insular loyalty to their little pack and sheer joy at doing what they feel in their bones is their job. His Whippet sighthound side added a new twist. When he ran down the disc and caught it, he gave it a violent shake. He had no idea why. A passing neighbor saw him do that and said, "He gets so happy when he catches it." I broke her heart and told her, "No, he doesn't understand, but he is breaking the neck of his prey." Is the chase or the kill the fun part for him? I don't know.

I give my heart to all my dogs, especially the ones who chose me as their person. Almost by accident every pair of dogs has neatly divided their primary relationships between my wife and me. Zoom is my dog. But I have that internal fortress. Even in my love of my dogs, I still had that hollow place they could not penetrate. I didn't let myself get all anthropomorphic with my dogs. Unabashedly affectionate, sure, but I didn't use the language or intent that they were somehow little people. My wife does that with ease. She embraces the whole 'doggie mama' thing. I mostly roll my eyes and don't question what she wants with the dogs. Zoom and I kept in our species lanes.

It started by accident. I was in my sitting in my desk chair putting on my shoes before leaving for work. When I finished putting on my shoes, Zoom came and bent his body in sort of a 'C' between my legs, leaning in with all his strength. I smiled, talked to him, and he stayed there until I felt the heat of his body through my pants legs. Dogs like rituals, predictability. In that, I am doglike. We began to do that little ritual every day. My other dogs always had long coats and sat between my legs at one time or another, but this was different. It wasn't close proximity that we both desired; it was contact, the warmth.

Zoom is a pure athlete, no fat, all muscle. Gangly and long, he can do a magic trick. Like a doggie origami, he pulls and folds all of his parts into a neat ball small enough to fit into my lap. I have a glorious old man's recliner and a couple of my dogs had jumped up to lay on it beside me, but this little guy came up and shrunk into a warm little ball between my legs while I read or watched TV. He is an insanely oversized lap dog. One night, he jumped up and laid on me with his head nuzzling the crook of my neck. I scratched his ear and he wrapped his front legs around my arm, crossing them to pull me closer. He let out a long sigh. I could feel his entire body relax into me as if he was suddenly overcome with a higher gravity than me. I stroked his face and said, "Little boy. You are my little boy dog." I had never had a male dog before; this was different. I had crossed a self-imposed boundary. I had let him in in a way no other creature had accomplished.

He taught me to let go of my confusion.

Something had shifted. I am not sure I was aware of it. I now talked to Zoom in ways that are, frankly, a little embarrassing. He snuggles my neck and I say things like, "There you go, little boy. That's where you belong." Now, when I yell, "Little Boy!" he comes running. Intensely curious about, well, everything, he is rarely more than a few feet away when I am writing, gardening, or building a fence. He lays on a blanket and watches me on the elliptical in the basement, waiting for me to lay down on the mat to do crunches so he can run over, jump on me and lay his head on my chest. If I am away for long, I miss the feel of him, the warmth and his smell. And all of this, all of this wonderfulness, scares the crap out of me. I am conscious every day that dog's lives are short. I have lived this loving contract with my dogs right to the last clause that says we will not let them suffer. Sometimes I am upset with myself that I have let this little dog get so far into my heart. But then I will be in another room for a while and he will push the door open, come over to me, nuzzle my hand, and put his paws in my lap so he can lick me once on my nose. I guess he missed me and merely wanted to know I was still there.

One night, as Zoom was laying on me and I was whispering in his ear that he was my little boy, my wife, sitting across the room, caught me doing it and smiled at me. I ducked a little, embarrassed, I guess, and she smiled again and said, "No, I love that. He has opened you up."

And there it was. I felt that sensation of openness right down to the core of my heart. The barricaded empty place that has always baffled me was full. I teared up when my wife said that and then she said, "Honey, that's a good thing." She is right. It is a good thing, an overwhelming and frightening loss of old boundaries. I now get it. Once you know that sensation, the fullness of love, there is no going back. I guess I finally had to learn that all along it was about seeking warmth, immutable warmth.

DIVE

―――――――――――――

LIKE MOST OLD MEN, I am capable of long lamentations about things that have been lost. I arrived in Portland during a deep economic recession. The state's timber industry had collapsed, and the city was years away from finding its economic footing. Almost nothing about the city was vibrant, especially in the inner neighborhoods that radiated east and west from the Willamette River. Still, there was a proud, blue collar feel to my first neighborhood, which suited me fine. On the arterial avenues on the inner east side, you could find anything you needed. Barbershops, porno palaces, all night restaurants, an espresso bar, laundromats, little drug stores, an all-night Mexican food joint, grocers, and most importantly, dive bars. As I had yet to find my own economic footing, I was especially fond of the dives. For a fifty-cent draft, I could escape my dingy little upstairs apartment and munch peanuts or popcorn while sitting at the bar watching the world go by and occasionally jotting my thoughts on cocktail napkins.

The avenues could feel a little rough at night. The assorted dive bars were dangerous by degree. In search of cheap entertainment, and mostly alone, I made a point of dropping by most of the bars within stumbling distance of home. Every bar had its regulars. Sometimes, in the morning, I'd drive by and see the residents of a bar waiting for the doors to open. They needed their first drink, second cigarette, and a bit of conversation with the morning paper. Likely as not, when I would drop by in the early evening, or even late at night, those same souls would be on station on *their* barstool or at *their* table.

Professional drinkers all, they never got drunk enough to be 86'd out of the bar. Functional inebriation. Conversations with their peers would be on a repeating loop of topics that never seemed to bore them. Always … always … one of the characters was the prettiest woman in an ugly bar. Much admired in her circle, her male peers vied for her attention. If I squinted, I could see the remnants of a great beauty washed away by time, whiskey, and cigarettes. I was pretty sure these regal women knew they lived just above the low bar for beauty in the dives they inhabited.

Mostly, I kept an ear perked, listening. Occasionally, I would inject myself into the closed circle conversations to punch my loneliness and see what would happen next. I have a knack for assuming the right persona for a place, so I was rarely shut down by the regulars. Mostly, I seemed to be a useful momentary addition to what they clearly saw as the family.

Being a night owl, I sifted through the options and began to end up at the same near empty dive for a nightcap. A few more bucks in my pocket now, before the explosion of microbreweries, meant I would land at one of two joints, a faux English pub and an ersatz Irish bar. They both had Guinness on tap, and most importantly, knew a proper pour. Likely as not, I would land on a barstool at the Irish dive called Biddy McGraw's. It was closest to navigate home if I indulged a shot with my beer. I never asked or cared who Biddy was. I went there for the floor show.

Being a nervous soul, I kept my truck parked in sight on the street outside; Biddy's was a strange choice. Danger was everywhere. This was the 1980s, 'The Troubles' were well afoot in Northern Ireland. There, pubs were being bombed and kneecaps were finding disciplinary bullets. Thousands of miles away, amidst the expat Irish brogues of the publicans and cooks, it was clear that Biddy's was an IRA bar. Mysterious things happened at a clearly off-limits to strangers table right next to the kitchen entrance. Posters in that corner of the room extolled the righteousness of the rebel cause and on one end of the table was a well-used collections box. Once I became recognizable to the crew, and showed I knew quite a bit about The Troubles, revelations began to flow. Seems that table was the Portland nexus for those who supported the IRA cause. The collection box was not only symbolic. When full, the money was routed to someone, somewhere, who would get the cash to someone else. The money went for needed 'supplies' … and then came the wink. Instruments of war was the implication. Once it was clear to me these folks were serious about their passions, I did more listening than questioning.

Meanwhile, often on the same nights, at the table under the front window nearest the front door was an entirely different collection of humanity. It was a time when cheap apartments could be found above the storefronts in my neighborhood. Right above Biddy's was the home (or was it the home base) of the core group of Portland's racist skinheads. Skinheads began as a right-wing group of toughs in England, a dangerous offshoot of the punk scene devoted to drinking, fighting, and racist intimidation. As such things do, the movement migrated in an organized fashion to America where they hooked up with the exuberant Klan and charmless Neo-Nazis. The gang in Portland was small. In our local punk scene, most of the violence was between the straight-edge, anti-racist punks and the skinheads. They lived to brawl with each other outside shows and bars. I had seen such trouble brew and skedaddled.

There was no mistaking the front table boys. Shaved heads, white power symbol tattoos, black pants bloused into Doc Martin books with red laces, bomber jackets over undershirts, and the ever-present suspenders, what the Brits call braces. The signal that a brawl was about to happen was when a combatant, 'dropped his braces,' meaning he pulled them over his shoulders and dropped them to his side. For any sane soul it meant … get the fuck out of there … run … fast.

I sat at the bar, closer to the IRA table than the front, but positioned where I could keep an eye on both. A skinny white guy sipping a beer, I was basically invisible, neither a target nor a friend. Occasionally, mid quaff, someone at the front table would look my way, do a scan, and slightly nod my way. Not worth his time was the verdict every time.

I was fascinated with the dynamics in the bar. I sat drinking, and in my head made up stories about who came and went from both tables. Like some dive bar sociologist, I fell comfortably back into one of my favorite places as the anonymous observer. It was better than sitting in my apartment with my epileptic Labrador watching what I could get on the antenna of my nine-inch black 'n white TV.

I know the exact moment I decided I was no longer going to hang out at Biddy's. I got the message in my morning newspaper. On a little hill a few blocks from my apartment, in the early morning hours, an African immigrant student at the local state university had the fatal misfortune to happen upon a carload of skinheads. Dragged from his car, he was beaten to death with baseball bats. I recognized the faces of the assailants as regulars at the front table.

Biddy's is gone but sometimes, as I am meandering around what is still my neighborhood, I will drive across that little knoll, look at the people walking by and think about the randomness of tragedy on that quaint little street. I wonder if those front table boys had dropped their braces. Probably not. It was never meant to be a fight.

MEMORY

———————————

I WROTE A MEMORY BOOK, not an autobiography. A memoir is not a disciplined retelling of one's life based on verified sources and in-depth interviews. I had considered talking to people across my life to confirm my memories, then rejected that approach. The book I offered is the product of what I recalled and what I discovered in decades of notes and letters. My wife rightly kept pushing me … why not ask someone? I still correspond with friends from different parts of my life; why not write them and see if my memory was correct? I came to believe that a memoir is the purest expression of self because it relies on only those events one can recall. The illusions, lies, and conceits we chose to embrace is the most refined version who we were and what we became.

To be sure, diving into the stacks of notes, journals, letters, cards, and pictures in my basement shook loose memories that had long ago receded from my consciousness. I was able to sequence events and sometime surprised myself. Sitting alone in the cool, damp air of my unfinished basement, I often said out loud, "Are you fucking kidding me; I did that?" Even then, those dislodged memories were still my own interpretation. Like a Seurat painting, I kept assembling little memory fragment dots into a picture with an utter disdain for the accuracies and inaccuracies. I am still not sure my approach was the best one, but I am convinced it was the right one.

Memory is a woven shawl. We weave a cloth, coarse and fine, and wrap the giant shawl around ourselves to keep us warm in a cold wind of reality. Because we all need this wrap of our memory, we fill in the missing or confusing parts lest we feel the chill through the gaps. When my book arrived in the hands of people I wrote about, they contacted me and said, "That's not how I remember that." Well, of course it isn't. Once, explaining to someone why I didn't spend more time confirming details, a curious explanation popped into my head.

Ever see the first *Jurassic Park* movie, the good one? The director, Steven Spielberg, had to solve a big problem. In Michael Crichton's book, the science is another character. He used detailed explanations of his take on genetic science to tell the reader how humans could create dinosaurs from DNA found in blood-sucking mosquitoes entombed in amber. I liked that geeky stuff. In the movie, Spielberg had to quickly get the audience up to speed. In a clunky sequence, the main characters are given a tour of the mysterious lab where the dinosaurs are birthed. One of the characters asks a white-coated scientist about the completeness of the DNA recovered from the ambered mosquitos. The too gleeful authority figure responded that there are gaps but that they found a universal cure. The filled the gaps with the DNA of a frog.

To write a memoir, any exploration of memory, you have to get comfortable with the fact that there are frogs everywhere. Though I have a very good memory, there were places where I vividly recalled my action or reaction but didn't have a clue about the catalyst or what happened next. Or … I recalled my answer to a question but not who asked it. If you remember the movie, it is using the frog DNA that leads to the frightening, violent unraveling of the Jurassic World theme park. Fortunately, I was able to contain the breeding, raging dinosaurs in my head until I gave them a safe world on the page.

About halfway through the first draft I realized that in order to create a coherent story I had to string together a deluge of stories with a common thread … my PTSD and Panic Disorder. I can't explain why I didn't see the obvious from the moment I wrote my first outline. How could I have missed that? I wrote the draft without a working title. If asked, I merely said "the writing project." After I had begun editing the manuscript, a title came to me while meditating—*Am I Cured Yet?* The editing was suddenly easier when I knew what the book was about, what story I really wanted to tell. Up until that point, I was acting on faith, the old 'things unseen.'

Now I knew which thread to pull every time I doubted the relevance of a word or a paragraph. Without my frogs, though, the story would have fallen into an incoherent stutter of disconnected moments. Generally, I used context, the nature of the people I wrote about, logic and guile, to keep the tale moving forward, the component parts of any good frog memory kit.

Everything in the memoir was working in context. I had written frogs to make it so. But one part didn't feel right. The story was about a Christmas eve trip I had taken to the Pacific coast and south-central Los Angeles. It was an important story because after college graduation it was the last gathering of my dearest friends. The trip included a Christmas eve visit to a good pal I didn't have a chance to say goodbye to at my graduation. The hospitality and sense of honor his Latino family showed me for visiting them on the day before the holiday touched me deeply. I was so swept away that I mostly missed Christmas eve with my own family. This was a favorite story I have told many times. But there was something wrong with the timeline. In the telling, my best friend Carl and I had flown home from Washington DC for Christmas, with the intent of taking a trip to LA. Carl, with whom I shared a house in DC, decided to skip the trip to LA. All of the contextual evidence worked. I had locked down the memory. I was ready to make my telling a permanent part of my memoir. But I was completely wrong.

One night, as I was falling asleep, I sat straight up in bed and said out loud, "No!" (My wife has long since given up remarking on these pre-sleep revelations.) I had a clear memory of driving to LA, and most importantly, what I was driving. I was in a pickup truck—my dad's. For my original frog to work, I would have been driving my little Toyota Corolla. I got out of bed and jotted a note. *Why wasn't I driving my own car?*

The next day, I looked at my note and knew the real story. I had moved the entire tale a year ahead. It was the wrong Christmas. Carl had gone to DC a year before me. It was Carl who flew home alone and reasonably decided not to leave his parents and go to LA. At that time, I was living in Salem, Oregon. Here's the strangest part. I had completely forgotten that I had flown down from Salem alone and that my car was still in Oregon. That is why I was driving Dad's truck. The graduation where I had missed my friend was not mine, but his, a year after mine. I had completely erased the flight from Oregon from my memory. I still can't remember anything about the flight, but now do recall being picked up at the airport by Carl and my old college roommate. All the time I was writing my subconscious had been working the problem. Something in the frog-filled telling of the story didn't ring true and it turned out that everything about the telling was completely wrong. All it took to correct the memory was to remember what I was driving. Too many damn frogs.

If I had not recalled that bronze colored Dodge pickup, my original story would have remained part of my memoir. I think, with time, I may have even become increasingly sure I had it right. Would that have been dishonest? Nope. That is now how our memory works. Focus on one memory, say from your childhood, and jot it down. Try to recall every detail. Unprompted, you will discover that your memory is full of frogs. Except in the case of hyperthymia, a syndrome where an individual is plagued by an almost complete, detailed autobiographical memory, we are all frog collectors.

Not remembering keeps us sane. There are moments and details that are best left permanently erased. Truth be told, so much of life is trivial that I wouldn't want all that junk hanging around for instant access. Do I really need to remember why I picked the blue socks this morning or which egg I picked from the carton for breakfast? Surely, that is the path to madness.

Sometimes, under stress, I preload memories. How is that even possible? I prepare to meet the world with monologues and dialogues in my head, brief and even detailed internal conversations. Days, weeks, even months ahead, I imagine scripts, sometimes saying them out loud, then I edit or amend them like a playwright. I create a memory before the actual moment happens. I practice what I intend to say, then anticipate the initial reaction and may even have entire alternate dialogues stored and ready depending on the real-time reaction. It's a way to sound confident, be witty, churn through my social anxiety, and hold people at arm's length. The real-world event is loaded with characters who have already been subject to my stage directions. I have built a social diving board, a jumping off place where I know the exact distance to the water of human interaction. But here's the problem. Most often reality doesn't vaguely resemble my preparation.

I wonder if sometimes my retained memory is more closely aligned with what I practiced with the inevitable *what I should have saids* rather than the reality. Have I become so comfortable with my practice dialogue that I no longer have the need to recall what actually happened? Have I molded my memory to conform with my expectation? Over time, it's entirely possible that my invented world, the story I tell over and over to myself and others has become the reality. Actually, it's more than possible; it's likely. This begs the question—am I lying? In many ways, all memory is a lie. There is no omniscient memory drone floating above us with a synaptic camera. We all muddle through, pick and choose what sticks in our heads.

As a PTSD survivor, I have a special relationship with memory. Trauma is a unique class of memory. Let me be clear, I am using the actual psychological definition of trauma as acts, or an act, that create lasting cellular changes, a deep imprint in the brain. The trauma can manifest itself without notice in a variety of frightening and baffling ways. In the current public discourse, the word trauma has been cheapened and abused. Day-to-day discomfort has been conflated with trauma to vitalize and aggrandize the trivial. No, hearing an opinion with which you disagree, even to the core of your being, is not a trauma. Societal harms leaking into your life are not traumas. The pop-psyche use of the word denigrates and demeans the many people around us who actually have PTSD. Need a referee for your claim of trauma? Talk to someone who has been diagnosed with PTSD. Someone who has committed to a lifetime of medication and treatment to live a 'normal' life. Find a soul who does not need a trigger to experience the physical and psychological manifestation of his trauma. He can have that experience suddenly appear wholly independent of the outside world in a biochemical fluttering of his mind or body.

My experience, one I have had confirmed by years of work with professionals, is that the memories installed by PTSD are inextricably linked to my body. There are movements and sensations that appear spontaneously when I have an episode related to my PTSD. Part of the therapeutic unwinding of the illness depends upon understanding and reinterpreting what it is my body wants to do when those deeply hidden memories come to the surface. Every case is unique. With consistent work, I uncovered a collection of incidents that got locked into my psyche. There was no single moment, no defining incident.

Consciously and unconsciously, I strain to create a psychic wall to keep the awful experiences from emerging. But here is where it gets tricky. Many times, in an attempt to make the past better, the most human defense is to replay the traumatic experience in my mind and body … over and over, and most horribly, completely out of context. We are resilient creatures, with a genetically coded imperative to take care of ourselves. In one way or another, everyone is a survivor. But when we get stuck in a memory, a popped balloon can cause a war veteran to assume a protective posture and unleash a preparatory flood of adrenaline. Part of the mind returns to the moment of damage and begs us to try once again to protect or repair ourselves. Except, out of context, the result is often more confusion and suffering. With practice, and sometimes medication, PTSD sufferers learn to manage the embarrassing and frightening physical manifestations, but behind their eyes the endocrine system is working overtime, muscles tense, heart rate up. Memory has them surrounded in a private hell of 'just in case.'

The old bromide is that 'time heals all wounds.' The physical body heals but the mind is different. Those wounds don't so much heal as drop from the synaptic priority list. Humans have a tendency toward a negativity bias. The bad stuff sticks. We chew it over and over with alarming ease, while recalling the good stuff takes more effort. We most naturally interpret the world around us as a collection of the annoying and awful. If the drive home from work is effortless Monday through Thursday, we will recall, and complain about, the traffic jam on Friday. The exception then becomes the rule and how we see commuting in general.

I wonder if my bias in my memoir was more negative because the thread I found and followed was based on my illness. Looking at the work now, there is a rhythm. In even the worst moments when I recount deaths, depression, and loss, I eventually turn to a redemptive story. The core belief of Buddhism is that life is suffering and the end of suffering. Within that belief system, the end of suffering does not just happen. It takes consciousness and effort. Could it be that the only stories I wrote are the ones where I, in the end, had something good to say? Are there many memoirs on the bookstore shelves that go something like: *My life was horrible and now I am now waiting for death in utter agony?* Not likely. It is entirely possible that as a memoirist, I have joined a self-selected collection of the self-absorbed and we can't let our stories end badly.

Memory permits each of us to be just honest enough. In any single telling, we will rewire or exaggerate our own stories, sometimes for comic effect or to layer some pathos on the less than interesting. Somewhere in there is the truth, but we are woefully limited creatures to relay what we saw or experienced with any real precision. Even if we take the time to triangulate the memories, borrowing the memory of others, we are caught in the Japanese director Akira Kurosawa's Rashomon dilemma, the blending of thought streams into a river of half-truth.

It works like this. One of my fondest childhood memories was my first family trip to the original Disneyland a few years after it opened. Decades on, at a family gathering, I told everyone that the one clear thing I still recall was of the enormity of the parking lots surrounding the amusement park. The rows of cars were so vast that little tractors pulled wagons full of expectant, happy visitors around the lot in constant circuits arriving at the front entrance. I said the ride on those wagons amongst the rows of cars was my favorite memory of the day.

My brother said, "But do you remember the most important thing Dad told us?"

"No," I responded, "I don't have a clue."

"Dad said for us to remember the letter and number of the row so we could get back to the car."

My brother couldn't recall the letter and number.

I can still see the wagons.

And Dad? He knew the letter but not the number.

CHIEF

THE TINY ROUND METAL TABLE was already overloaded with six empty beer bottles and assorted crumpled balls of cocktail napkins. She had waved away the offer of glasses. We met at the little bar beneath the office tower where I was currently robbing an insurance company as a consultant. I beat her there. She had pedaled up on her bike, shook my hand, and hung her helmet from the back of the spindly chair.

"Hi Jim, I'm Betsy," she said, "IPAs?"

I first heard about Betsy as one of the 'Big Four' on Commissioner Nick Fish's first, heartbreaking loss in his 2004 run for Portland City Council. As the rookie policy wonk on Nick's new 2008 campaign, I was looking for help wherever I could get it. I reached out to the veterans of the previous effort, but quickly learned that the loss the first time around had been so surprising and devastating that while supportive, the former crew was going to mostly sit this new campaign out.

Win or lose, few things end so completely, or suddenly, as a political campaign. From frenzy to silence in minutes. I came back to the headquarters the day after the election and sat by myself in the empty room surrounded by the now useless remnants of a victory. Posters, shiny mailers, phone lists, precinct maps, empty pizza boxes, and cold, half-empty cups of coffee.

After winning the election, Nick had chosen to bring in more experienced people for his City Hall staff. I was crushed not to be there, but quickly used my old information technology connections to land a boring consulting gig and refill the bank account. I hated the work but cashed the checks.

By all accounts, Nick's first year as a commissioner was chaotic. During the campaign I learned that he had the scary ability to go at the same speed in ten different directions at once and the first city hall team simply couldn't contain or harness his boundless energy. A year on, a second version of his team was forming, with Betsy as Chief of Staff.

I was hand tremor nervous waiting for Betsy. Not knowing the protocol, I held off ordering a drink. When I left my long IT career the first time, it was my intent to fulfill two lifelong dreams. First, be on the inside of a winning political campaign, and second, be the invisible guy in the back of the room, part of a team governing. Sitting outside on a lovely night, I knew this was my last shot to fulfill my dream.

The first beer calmed me. I told the already tiresome to me tale of why I had abandoned a twenty-four-year career to change my life. She told me stories from the first Fish campaign and about her jobs at the City. We both shared our obsessive love for our dogs. That night, Betsy was funny, in a curiously restrained way. Her laugh could boom but then she caught it in her throat, lest it go too far. Fair skinned, her face turned deep red when she shared insider stories about the first Fish campaign or when she was saying anything the least bit conspiratorial. No poker player she. But's here's the thing, one beer in, we were already a team. What we were doing wasn't an interview at all. We were just two nerds hanging out, telling tales.

Finally, as the fourth round arrived and I was getting a little tipsy, I said, "So … Betsy … what are we doing here?"

Her laugh boomed and she turned red again.

"Oh. Oh, I forgot to ask you. Do you want to come to City Hall with me and work for Nick?"

I laughed with her.

"I am having a good time here, but I was hoping that was the point. Of course!" An electric shot went through my body and I fought to contain a crack in my voice and welling eyes. She offered one third of the salary I had made in my old IT job and I was delighted.

In my work life, I have had bosses, peers, and teams working for me. But my two years with Betsy in City Hall was different. In the political world, almost all relationships are transactional. I quickly got annoyed by how often the word 'friend' gets tossed about and how little it actually means. When, after two years, Betsy moved on to another job at the city, I thought about what our work together had been. While I hesitated to say it out loud because it sounded so strange, I arrived at the conclusion that ours was the most intimate working relationship I had ever had.

The years had caught up to me and for the first time I had a boss who was more than a decade younger than me. But what was immediately clear was that Betsy (I called her

Bets) and I shared an important skill and a preference. We were both systems people, her from her city work and me from decades in a big corporation. We both could look at a tangled mess of bureaucracy and policy then, mostly in our heads, deconstruct it in ways that would help our boss, the commissioner, who, for all his considerable skills, had no experience or understanding of big systems. Behind closed doors, back and forth in each other's offices, we strategized and schemed, always focused on how to help our boss be better at his job.

The preference was an agreement that mornings sucked. Her with her coffee, me with my tea, we merely tolerated all that horrible morning energy around us until our brains caught up with our bodies. But on the backend of the day, we both reveled in the quiet hours when everyone else was gone and it was the two of us. Our conversations slowed down, mixing both the personal and professional. Still, no matter how long I stayed, she was at her desk when I waved goodbye.

We had great fun trying to provide a semblance of order for the team. Gradually, sometimes subversively, we succeeded. Whether in shifting the organization or creating a policy initiative, there was always the moment when we had to pitch the idea to Nick. Back behind a closed door again, almost always in my office as it didn't adjoin the Commissioner's, we set up our tag team. I am a natural antagonist, so I often made the pitch followed quickly by Betsy as the deeply experienced, wise insider. When my change agent routine began to wear thin with Nick, we would switch roles. Nick mostly knew he was being played but I think he gave us more space to push hard because both Betsy and I had been in the trenches for his campaigns. In politics, shared scars count for something.

I was in my happy place. Almost every morning as I walked into the building, I looked up at the little brass sign that said City Hall and smiled. But after two years, mission accomplished, Betsy was ready to disconnect from the endless demands of being our Chief of Staff. For a parting gift, I gave her an actual travel case for her beloved iPad to replace the ratty sack she used. Then I did something I knew was hard for her to take.

I said, "Okay, now you're going to have to endure this."

I gave her a hug.

Betsy returned to her most natural environment, the complex wheels and cogs of the bureaucracy of city government. If you have the right eyes, it is impossible to live in Portland without seeing something Betsy made. Her ideas, the fruits of her management savvy, and her passion for her home is everywhere around us.

Betsy lived to travel. She had her office walls remade as giant cork boards where she stuck hundreds of pictures of the places she visited. The entire time I knew her there was never a moment where she was not planning the next trip. Even when the cancer appeared, she didn't let up, arranging chemo in Mexico, and crossing North Africa off her itinerary list.

Something else Bets and I shared: as introverts we wrote our way through life. She blogged about her cancer. I read the long, frighteningly detailed posts with a sense of awe and wonder. She applied her remarkable eye to every nuance of her body, medical care, and the loving people around her. Some may want to say the writing was courageous but that isn't it. It was as if she was using all her considerable powers of observation and organization in an attempt to write the cancer into submission.

Two weeks before cancer finished its evil work, there was a retirement celebration in City Hall for Betsy. She had taken a year-long leave of absence but finally knew she had to retire. I still had a little trouble walking into City Hall after the pain of my own departure from the building. But I needed to be there. I slipped in early and as she was getting settled, snuck up front and said, "Hi Boss," and gave her a hug. She didn't smile; kept moving forward. It was clear that being there was both an act of will and love. The speeches were lovely and there was a concerted attempt to bring joy to the tall atrium. Still, I was struck that what I was seeing was not unlike a memorial service with the person being remembered in the room. I don't think that as so much morbid as remarkable. Few people get that moment. Her determination, pure Betsy, had put her in that room.

At the end, Betsy took the microphone. Seated, clearly exhausted, the medication robbing her of continuity of thought, she made it clear to us all that this was a 'disability retirement.' She did not want to go. She talked about time, the time she had, which she haltingly measured in years "one … two or three." But knowing Betsy, she wasn't fooling herself at all. I think she said that for all of us. Then, in one line, she was completely there for us to see. She looked across the room at her longtime partner, David.

"He may be an asshole … but he's my asshole."

We laughed. That was Betsy expressing love.

As I have grown older and lost people in my life, I keep looking for solace, finding it occasionally. When the message I knew was coming appeared in my email, it came from her sister. I once again fell upon the Jewish blessing: May her memory be a blessing.

Bets, I am blessed.

SIT

I REJECTED THE BIG THREE RELIGIONS. I was looking for something that was both psychologically sustaining and funny or at least imbued with a deep appreciation of irony. Christianity, Islam, and Judaism are mind-numbingly serious. God is so demanding. I grew up in Christianity (Southern Baptist … yikes.) and spent years studying the other two. My experience of the committed believers is that they have chosen to have their irony gene removed. To revel in a torrent of judgment and call that love is perhaps the most ironic choice one can make. They don't see it. So, I cast a wider net. Well, not so much casting a net as falling off the pier into the ocean and realizing that I was just one of the fish.

I am plagued by an inner voice, one that judges and cajoles and classifies … well … everything I see and everyone I meet. That little inner voice isn't so much the voice of god, or even my own voice; it sounds a lot like Groucho Marx shooting an endless stream of one-liners in an ever-revolving series of set-ups and punch lines. For a few decades, Groucho was the acerbically witty narrator and conductor for the Marx Brothers. He had the uncanny, if frightening, ability to slice a pompous person to bits in ways that left the victims laughing at their own demise. At funerals, in deeply serious meetings, with family and especially in the midst of strangers I can't stop seeing the world around me as essentially funny. There is a constant battle between the exterior Jim, appropriate to the moment, nodding in agreement or concern, and the inner one who is amusing himself by twisting every instant to alleviate boredom. The worst social pits I have ever had to climb out of were inevitably dug when I lost tight hold of my wisecracking inner Groucho.

I have one Groucho Marx story that acts as a guidepost. Doesn't everyone? The desert where I grew up is littered with country clubs and golf courses. All sorts of celebrities have homes in the Palm Springs desert area. Weird celebrity sightings were commonplace. One night, at a stoplight in my buddy's faded yellow VW bug, happily stoned, I looked at the car next to me and saw a familiar ski jump shaped nose. It was connected to the Bob Hope. He smiled, gave me a 'cheerio' wave and sped away from the light in his giant Ford Thunderbird. The moment was strangely normal.

Somehow, another of my pals had discovered the home address of Groucho Marx. The American icon lived in a typical, sprawling ranch home on a public street, not inside the gates of a country club like so many of his contemporaries. Bored, one night some of my friends made a collective decision to go to Groucho's house and knock on his door. There was no intent to harass him or behave in any disrespectful way. I think it was simply a matter of proving that the most famous Marx Brother lived there.

The ringleader, the one who found out the address, was a smallish, Nisei Japanese-American named Dennis. Thick glasses, long shoulder length hair, he was our version of a stoner intellectual. No one else had the audacity to go up to the assumed Marx Brother front door. Dennis was our representative. No hesitation, he walked right up and rang the doorbell. Almost immediately, the door opened and there was the man. Small, in his trademark beret, he stood eye to eye with our diminutive friend. Dennis was speechless.

Groucho cocked his head and said, "You're short. Go away." And with that closed the door in our buddy's face. Now we knew, for a fact, where Groucho Marx lived.

Groucho was my guru. His rapid-fire quips are essentially how my mind works … all … the … time. Wit is my verbal sword and shield. I can make people laugh or scratch their heads in confusion with a quickly tossed off sentence. Pushed by someone who is hostile or a bully, humor is my weapon of choice, especially if I can get a laugh at the expense of the offender. I love the power of easily twisting words with a straight face like Groucho with his flip of ash off the tip of his ever-present cigar.

In my forties, I made a final attempt to reconcile with religion by joining my wife in becoming a member of the Unitarian Universalist Church. The UUs, as they call themselves, are a kind and sincere bunch. In Portland, the already liberal bent of the church takes a jarring lurch farther to the left. I had hoped that their attempt to de-dogmatize Christianity would be a spiritual fit for me. Truth be told, I was looking less for a religion than a set of shared ethical organizing principles. It didn't take long for me to figure out that they were on the right track by taking the white, bearded Christian God down to size, but in the place of that unifying figure they had chosen to ramp up the dogma for everything else. Liberalism was the actual religion and the unifying source of their very un-Groucho evangelical fervor.

After the Sunday service, people retired downstairs to a big room for stale cookies, bad coffee, and rows and rows of cause tables. UUs are joiners. When they are not stopping wars, they are knitting socks for the homeless or saving the planet from meat by passing out vegan recipes. No doubt the causes represented were good ones. Unfortunately, inner Groucho was very excited. It was a target rich environment as I can't stop myself from questioning everything and have never been one to "join" anything.

Nothing makes a UU happier than a cumbersome, committed failure to reach consensus, the precise thing that drives me nuts. My proverbial camel's straw was a campaign against war that entreated people to bring little toy soldiers so that they could be randomly distributed around the city to protest one of our perpetual wars. When I asked if anyone had considered that their plan actually demonized the young people who chose to serve their country, it didn't go well. Nothing riles up the self-anointed tolerant more than having someone point out their intolerance. I defaulted to Groucho: "I don't want to be part of any club that will accept me as a member."

But one thing that UUs did stuck with me. Under the unifying 'no God' banner were evening breakout groups that dove deep into what they achingly labeled 'spiritual traditions.' Irony suspended; people gathered to fill the spiritual hole at heart of the UU body with bits of other religions. My inner Groucho was egging me on to tell people how hilarious I found this. Exercising my sometime adultness, I didn't say a thing and went ahead and signed up for a mindfulness meditation class. Caught in my own irony loop, I was hoping to silence, if only for a moment, my busy mind and chronic muscle twisting anxiety.

One night, a Soto Zen Monk showed up to teach us the meditation method of his order. I was impressed at the audacity of a 6-foot 4-inch white guy roaming the streets in a dark brown robe and sandals. *Here's a guy who doesn't give a damn about peer pressure*, I thought. After his lecture, I was still confused about his meditation method. I asked him an earnest question about his 'technique.' And here's the thing that went right to my inner Groucho, the smart-alecky twist I had been waiting for all my life; the unexpected shot to my psyche. Without pausing, he looked me in the eye and said, "Just sit." Then, a slight, flat-lipped smile and he walked away.

I didn't say anything in response, but inner Groucho fell over laughing. "Of course, you idiot, just sit," Groucho said. I had been topped, put in my place with two words. No complexity. Just sit your ass down, and when you are done, stand up. Damn, these Zen Buddhists are funny, and they don't mess around. I stopped being a Unitarian in a second. Enlightenment without walking the road to Damascus.

Then I made it hard. Of course, I did. In my usual delightfully obsessive way, I dove into a study of Zen. Books, tapes, documentaries. I ordered a zafu and zabuton (meditation pillow and mat) from the monk's main temple. When the sitting kit didn't arrive in a few weeks, I called the monastery to see what the delay was all about. The answer, "We've been meditating." Holy shit these guys are the good! I acquired Buddha statues—big and small—and went to local priory for more meditation instruction. But it was there, on the third night, that I ran smack into my old problem. The sangha (congregation) of the priory and the monks spent a lot of time talking about joining them, and to my chagrin, it turned out they saw Zen Buddhism as a religion. They weren't so much evangelical as gently persuasive that the whole Zen practice is better if you do in a group, and oh, show up to clean the temple and tithe. I finished the training and never went back. I would find my own way to study Zen and do what I really wanted to do: just sit.

And for almost two decades, that is exactly what I did. Every night I sit, even when I am sick. I had asked one of the monks what they do when they have a cold. "Still sit," she said. Yeah, still only two words. All she needed was a cigar. At some point, being a nerd and in violation of all the precepts of Zen, I got a phone app to time my evening meditations, mostly to do as they did at the priory, ring a bell to begin and one to end the session. Except, being an app, it tries to make you part of a world community of meditators. Somehow, I was okay with that as I would never actually meet any of those folks. Still a radical introvert, it was kind of nice to know I wasn't the only one making this up as I went along. The app keeps a running total of when you sit how long you have meditated. I mostly ignored that total number of hours until I started writing this essay. Turns out I have been just sitting, cross-legged and staring at a wall for about 38,000 minutes. I'll do the math for you. I have meditated for something over twenty-six days, almost a month of my life. What? How did a guy who discards hobbies as soon as he figures them out ever end up doing that? Inner Groucho interjects, "Because Zen has a joke book."

Zen teaching is, in part, people relaying century's old little stories called koans. These are often stories of how people became 'enlightened.' There are hundreds of books that attempt to describe enlightenment but for my purposes I'll simplify: "Oh! Now I get it!" *It* being the fundamental teachings of Buddhism. The personal experience of the newly enlightened is sometimes told as the equivalent of having someone hit you upside your head. There is actually a Zen order where a monk walks around with a stick while the other monks are meditating. Start to nod off and he clobbers you. Seriously, actual slapstick. The Marx Brother's movie *Horse Feathers* in brown robes.

There are thousands of koans but this one will give you the idea.

~

Once a monk made a request of Joshu.

"I have just entered the monastery," he said. "Please give me instructions, Master."

Joshu said, "Have you had your breakfast?"

"Yes, I have," replied the monk.

"Then," said Joshu, "wash your bowls."

The monk was enlightened.

~

There isn't an inch of difference between "Then wash your bowls," and "You're short. Go away." Like Groucho's best one-liners, a koan is supposed to make you furrow your brow while laughing. The most common reaction to a koan is to ask, "What?" Could anything be better for a guy suffering inner Groucho Marx syndrome than having the entire point of a religious practice be trying to figure out the punchline of a joke?

We all have these annoying little inner voices constantly tell us things. Some people think they hear the voice of God. You know, the angel on one shoulder, the devil on the other. But even in that formulation, in the center lies personal choice. My voice happens to be a dead, twentieth century singer and comedian who came to fame making people laugh during the Great Depression. I have no idea how that happened. If your inner voice is only you, then I am sorry. It's a lot more fun when it's a comedian. Considering what people's inner voices sometimes tell them to do, I think I got pretty lucky.

If you were to sit down and make a list of the chance things that permanently changed your life, I am guessing the list would be a short one. Oh, you can plan things like a marriage, maybe a birth, even anticipate a death. But if you honestly trace the origins of the planned things you will discover the unplanned catalyst. Once, sleeping on a couch in the work break room, I opened my eyes to see my future wife's socks, only the socks, and thought they were very cool. I asked her out because I loved her socks. Yeah, those kinds of random epiphanies with lasting impact. It is impossible to know what moments among the daily cascade of events, people, and words will be indelible. So many little things have to align for you to hold a memory dear, and beyond that, have that memory change the course of your life, thus having a rippling impact on everyone around you. I had this strange voice in my head waiting for a cosmic punchline. Was I enlightened when a robed monk told me, "Just sit?" Maybe. I don't know. But it was damned funny.

SPEED

_____

I WROTE MY MEMOIR IN A RUSH. Words cascaded day after day for almost six months. Sometimes I felt like I was at the keyboard transcribing thoughts as fast as I could lest they suddenly disappeared. I woke up compelled and joyful to be writing. One thousand words appeared almost effortlessly. Some days, chasing the muse, I wrote three times that until my fingers ached and my hands felt slightly numb. The music I played only enhanced the sense of forward motion. I fired up Spotify channels of repetitive, urging, minimalist composers: Phillip Glass and John Adams. I emptied out the music queues and started over at the top. Music with no words to break into my mind, almost random notes swirling around me turned up loud. When the subject I was writing went to my broken emotional core, and I was crying while typing, I kept at it. Some days I wrote to exhaustion, then had to take the next day off or throw a Frisbee for my dog or walk off in any direction. But the breaks were a short pause. Soon I was back, furiously slinging words.

Quite on purpose, I spent no time learning how to write a memoir. A friend suggested a seminar but that seemed bizarre to me. Beyond going through decades of my own notes and correspondence, the only conscious preparation I did was to reread Hunter S. Thompson's *Fear and Loathing in Las Vegas* and John Steinbeck's *Travels with Charley in Search of America*. Thompson's writing is the essence of ferocious forward motion and freed my mind from the need for perfect narratives. He pushes and pushes and pushes, then slaps you upside the head with a paragraph of insightful, beautiful prose that can bring you to tears. Steinbeck is a master of narrative storytelling. Each chapter is a new place with new people, and of course, a dog runs through it. Those two books were my classroom. I needed to trust that my subconscious had been working on the project for a lifetime. The first draft ended up with almost three times as many words as I needed to tell my story. Then began editing with the same aggressive energy. Every day, I rejoiced in the word count going down as much as I had been obsessed with it going up. Up. Down. As long it was moving in either direction, I was elated. Moving that number became its own motivation. Primal productivity. Instant reward.

But once I held my first book in my hands, I began to wonder why I was in such a frenzy. Why the need for speed? What was my hurry?

Speed can be the mother of focus. I learned this in a car on a racetrack. Driving at your limit, every upward tick of the speedometer means that the penalty for a bauble or hesitation increases. I spent some time with my hot little Mini Cooper S on a racetrack. Track days are euphemistically called Performance Driving Education. That's true. No one who has only driven on legal roads will ever truly know how to drive a car. I suppress a giggle when people go on and on about how good of a driver they are. Compared to what?

Growing up going to stock car races and a longtime fan of the pinnacle of performance racing, Formula One, I was forever curious about what it felt like to drive a car to its potential. Any car. Oh, I had found empty stretches of road, stomped down the gas and watched as the speedometer climbed over 100 miles per hour. People do that all the time, but speed in a straight line isn't a challenge. It's going fast, briefly and pointlessly. What an embarrassment when someone doing that wraps the car around a tree and is killed. Dead is bad enough, but dead and dumb, oh the ignominy.

To challenge one's ability to control a car, you have to drive a road course with high speed braking and turns. A track day is designed to tell you how little you know about driving a car. This is how it works. First, you hand a credentialed organization a pile of dough. Enough to show your commitment to the concept. Early in the morning you line up your car to have it inspected. Safety is the watchword. But it is what the inspectors are looking for that gets your attention. You will get dinged for "loose items" anywhere. Even in your trunk. If it can fly about, it can distract you at the wheel. All the mechanical things—tires, brakes, oil, fuel—are obvious. But my inspector had me make sure my car battery was tightly screwed down and that the terminals weren't exposed. "Don't want it flying out and sparking a fire." What? *That's a thing? What have I gotten myself into?*

In theory, any car can do a track day. But in reality, I was among my people … car geeks who, like me, made sure their car looked as good as possible in the line-up. To intimidate us rookies, there were experienced race drivers in fast street cars they had modified with special tires and track ready configurations. Because we were put into groups based on experience, none of the novices, like me, would be on the track at the same time with the real speedsters. They had all the gear—driving suits and shoes, their own helmets and gloves. My first time renting a helmet I bought a balaclava to keep my sweat from salty lines already in the helmet lining. You don't put a wheel on the track without a helmet.

Each novice was assigned an experienced race driver to ride shotgun. My first coach was an older gentleman, a veteran of club racing, who during our introduction told me about recently putting his BMW M3 into the wall on a track up north. He was fine and brought his super tuned Mini Cooper to the track that day instead. I thought, *Uh, I only have this one car*.

Almost everything you know about driving a car is meaningless on a track. Morning training started with studying apexes, FIA curbing, the racing line, wave-through passing, tire contact patches, weight transfer, breaking points, turn-in points, car rotation, and all the actions that could get you banned from the track completely. I suppose the most important takeaway from all of that is that there is one fastest way around the almost two-mile track. Do everything right, stay in that racing line, and you will be fast. I would have four twenty-minute sessions on the track to learn how to do that.

As my teacher and I strapped into the car, I was immediately taken by how disorienting a helmet was. The weight on my head. The restricted vision. The sense you are looking out of a little tunnel at the world. But there was no time to adjust as the starter waved a green flag and a marshal pointed me onto the track. The first novice session was limited to a maximum of 80 MPH. Reasonable, except for the immediate sensory overload. Windows down, wind rushing into the car, my coach was yelling instructions from the first corner. "Too Deep! Turn in Now! Brake Now! Too late on that shift?! Brake here to get weight on the front tires! Good! Missed that apex! Go ahead and hit the curbs! Are your brakes fading?! Closer to the wall! There you go! You can get closer! Downshift sooner! Keep your RPMs up! Your car will hold that turn, trust it! Don't pay attention to the tires squealing, that's a good sound!" My inner dialogue was pretty basic, something along the lines of "Shit! Shit! Shit!"

We pulled back into the pits. I parked the car and he said, "Don't use your parking brake. Your brakes are hot enough to weld the pads to the drum. Open the hood of your car to help cool it down." He stepped away and came back with a bottle of cold water and a power bar. "Drink the whole thing and eat this; I'll be back for the next run at full speed." *Full speed*, I thought?

I was intoxicated on rapidly fading adrenaline and followed his orders. I then lay down under a tree and dosed off for a few minutes. Even at a slower speed, the entire experience was a blur. It felt like I didn't know how to drive at all. In order to follow my coach's instructions, I had to ignore every rational impulse I have ever had as a driver. He told me to brake way later and harder than my foot wanted. The sound of screaming tires told me to slow down, but he said push harder into the corner. Former 'safe' distances from walls and other cars were now simply wrong. But under all my confusing was the kernel of a new truth. I could do this. I was in control. This was fun. And most astonishingly, I thought, *This is like my Zen meditation. To do this I have to stay completely in the moment, excluding all other thoughts*. It was wonderful.

Session after session, I got faster. I learned that the faster I drove, the less my coach talked. My connection to my car became more natural and I stopped thinking about the basics and began to actually see the racing line. Each lap was a challenge. In all the times I did track days, I never did my perfect complete lap. I always made mistakes. What I learned was that when I got a corner, or a complex right, it was like soaring. The car seemed to float on the track, smooth and connected. Every other thought vanished because my safety and my pursuit of little moments of perfection was dependent on complete focus. When everything was working, speed actually slowed me down. My senses aligned with my singular action.

I was only frightened once all day. In the final track session, I was tired. I hadn't anticipated how physically taxing driving at speed would be. Professional race car drivers are amazing athletes. In one hard corner I was probably experiencing 1G, the effect of one times gravity laterally. I felt like my heavy, helmeted head wanted to fly out of the passenger window. Race drivers experience five times G Force in two-hour races.

Tired, getting a little too comfortable, I was at over 100 MPH on the back straight approaching a complex of turns. I was looking at the braking zone signs that help you figure out when to stomp on the brakes. I was at the 400-foot sign.

I had learned to brake just beyond the 300. It is an oddity of Portland International Raceway that there is a lake and natural area in the middle of the track. Fast cars actually protect the birds from encroachment. When I looked the 400-foot sign, my eyes shifted for a millisecond and I had the thought: *Trees.* Just that one word, 'Trees.' In the same second, my mind began yelling at me, *No trees! No trees! No trees! BRAAAAAKE!* Somehow, even more adrenaline pumped into my system. I made the corners but was way wide toward the wall in the final turn into the front straight. I had broken my track Zen. When we came to a stop my coach said, "Good session. I am going to approve you for solo driving next time you come. But I wondered what you were going to do with that wall in the last corner. That would have hurt if you hit it," he said laughing as he shook my hand.

As I wrote my book, I believed it was possible to overthink my own story. Like driving fast, it seemed to work best when I let go of intentionality. We are all our own editors. Speed had the virtue of unleashing the rawest first draft of my memories. Holding to a commitment to myself, in the editing that followed I clung to each truth over embarrassment or deflection. I understood the effect of looking away at the trees, that I would flinch and subsequently lose the thread, the race line.

Perhaps an even more primal reason for my speed was death. Chapter after chapter, at the end of the day, I wondered *"What would happen to all this work if I suddenly died?* Having committed to the memoir, finishing it took on a greater urgency. *If I got hit by a bus, could my wife figure out my confusing collection of chapters.* Standing at my desk, I had changed how I organized and named the raw product of my days many times. It would baffle anyone attempting to open the cabinet drawers in my mind. There were notes on my whiteboard, on legal pads, and littered in all sorts of files on my Mac or on thumb drives. I had spontaneous musings on my phone and cryptic yellow sticky notes on my old journals. No one could make sense of that craziness. More importantly, would anyone care to try? The hubris well fills quickly for the memoirist.

The book became a repository for my stories. Without children, I had no one to tell all the generations of stories I had collected or created. The recent passing of people younger than me was a stark reminder that we don't get to decide when the story collecting and telling stops. I thought about that fat first draft and all the stories I cut to get to the final book with some reassurance. Well, I thought, at least those stories are recorded somewhere, hidden in an early draft; at least if others were curious and persistent, they could recover what will be completely lost when I am hot gasses floating up out of a crematorium chimney. As my memories became tangible as electrons, words on a page, I found I could breathe a little easier. A friend, in a moment of honesty, told me he had kids to keep the genetic code going. Yeah, I got that, compelled to protect the line in a human attempt at immortality. Having made the choice not to pay my genes forward, one of the compelling reasons to write and write as fast as I could was to create my own version of a genetic code. One that someone could read by candlelight during the apocalypse.

While working on even the hardest, darkest stories, I remained compelled forward with the sheer joy of the writing. I didn't feel like I could let up. A memoir isn't a closed system. I was always surrounded by my assumed readers. Over the course of a lifetime, there were people who in the writing came back to life in the room with me.

For some, I was writing an apologia, others an explanation, and still others a warm embrace. This host of ghosts were my companions and once I committed to them, I woke each day worried that not completing my tome would let them down. Especially present for me was my father.

Dad is the last of the line of his generation of Blackwoods. People at my juncture of life become acutely conscious of the fragility of the generation hovering above them on the family tree. In recent visits home, right before and after my mom succumbed to Alzheimer's disease, my father had been unloading family history in large chunks. Hundreds of photographs were sorted and explained. Black and white, grainy pictures of people only he was still able to name and place in context. My brother, who lives near to Dad, was the primary recipient of this burden and blessing. When I flew down to visit, I took in as much as one can in a sitting. My writing became the reciprocal part of this imparting of hidden knowledge. There were things I wanted Dad to know and understand, and most essentially, for us, there was suffering I wanted to relieve.

As much as my own death, I considered my father's inevitable passing as fuel for the speed of my writing. With the motivation of impermanence in the room, I pushed ahead. My need to give my story, our story, to my dad meant he saw a manuscript draft even before my beta readers. Rough, over-long and in some places still loosely held together, I emailed a copy to him with a great sense of relief. He would have to read it on his computer as it was too large for him to print. His eyes are not what they used to be, so I bumped up the font size. Relieved, I went back to my editing. I figured it would take weeks for him to wind his way through that fat draft.

Speed begat speed. On the second day after he got the manuscript, Dad called to tell me he had finished it. Over 350 pages in that incarnation, I could not believe that was possible. He said that once he started, he didn't stop reading. Apple meet the tree. He said he saw a lot of things he recognized and there were things he remembered differently … of course. I had months of work still to do but now I could exhale. Dad had seen it.

At last, I could slow down. Over the next months, on my own and working with my new editor, I could simply and joyfully focus not on the work as arm wrestling a speeding existential crisis, but as an endless number of fun problems to solve. I could finally slow down.

MISSING

I MUST HAVE BEEN around eight-years-old. My little brother and I were staying with our maternal grandparents. They lived out at the ranch. For the rest of the world, a ranch in parts of the southwest is a farm. The ranch grew citrus and table grapes. The whole ranch thing is a hangover from the Mexican ranchero. Grandma had driven us to town for some groceries. At the Thrifty store, the big treat for us was an ice cream cone. The scoops weren't like any other ice cream store. The clerk used a device that looked like a tube with a pistol grip. She plunged it into the tub of ice cream, pulled the device out hard, then ejected the cylindrical rocky road onto the sugar cone. I was sure we got more ice cream at Thrifty because of that strange device.

Grandma Lois had a full cart but needed one more essential item. Thinking back, it was probably the real reason we went to the store at all. Grandpa was out of wine, red wine. Against a wall up front were stacks of half open boxes of gallons of Gallo wine. Grandpa bought his wine a gallon at a time. Grandma pushed the cart in front of the stacks and stared at the bottles. My brother and I licked our ice cream and watched Grandma. She seemed to be frozen. Her face was scrunched up in worry, mouth closed, lips stretched thin, lines at the edges of her eyes more deeply furrowed. I walked closer.

She said to me, "Your grandpa has a favorite. He only likes one kind but there are two different red wines. I can't remember which one he wants."

She fingered the bottles back and forth, picked one up to look closer at the label.

"I don't know. He won't like it if I get the wrong one."

She considered the bottles long enough for me to be down to the cone, crunching on the edges.

"Oh, I don't know … I don't know," she said.

Some kids understand fear early on. We know what it feels like when we are afraid, and we have seen what it looks like when a dog or a cat skitters away in fear. I didn't understand why those big bottles of wine scared my grandma, but I could tell she was afraid. Frozen fear. I tried to help.

"I think Grandpa likes that one," I said pointing at a bottle with no real knowledge, only the intent to try to alleviate my grandma's fear.

"You think so?" she said, hopefully.

"Yeah, Grandpa will like that one."

And there my memory ends. I know two bottles went into the cart. I know we left. I don't recall a thing after that.

I wrote an entire memoir without mentioning my mom's parents. They died months apart in 1980. I was living on the east coast. Unable to travel, I wrote memorials of my grandparents that I sent to my mom. Like many memories, these details were lost only to be restored when we emptied the contents of my mother's safe years after her death. Now I have the funeral cards for my grandparents' services and the words I sent home. I typed my memorials on a type of paper lost to time. Corrasable Bond paper feels like parchment and has some sort of surface coating that allows one to erase the typewriting with barely a trace. It also smudges too easily so the finished pages need to be gently caressed and held by the edges. Always a horrible typist, this pentimento paper was my go-to in collage and beyond until the invention of the computer keyboard and the all-powerful backspace key. I'm blessed with a rapid-fire little finger on my right hand to tap away my typing blunders. I didn't date either eulogy. I am not sure why but for decades I didn't date anything I wrote, even journals. I suppose I thought I would remember when I wrote things. The muddle of the temporary hubris of my youth is a large timeless mound of paper.

Mom died a slow, awful death; first of her mind and much later her body. Dementia. Going through her things, it is clear she anticipated her disappearance. Everywhere in the bits of her life are helpful notes, dates, and directions. Not even my dad knows when she started curating her life like this. She always had a mother's sense of generational time. I think she hoped that someone would care. More likely, as the keeper and chronicler of stories, I think she knew that one day I would care. I think she would be happy to know how much I care and how hard I work with these pieces of her life to tell more stories.

On top of each of the yellowed remembrances is a blue sticky note. In her clear cursive hand, she wrote on each one: *Written by Jim Blackwood, Jr.* The notes were found next to the neatly labeled funeral cards. Again, she didn't write dates, so I'll never know when she did all this archival work. For every bit of clarity we leave in our wake, we also leave a thousand mysteries. The ratio is startling.

Grandma died first, in March. An epic family story became part of the day she died. My grandparents lived in Buckeye, Arizona, then a small enclave to the west of Phoenix, since gobbled up by the megalopolis. They lived in a mobile home parked next to a huge, handmade trailer full of tools and a welder. Grandad was a fabricator. Metal, wood, he could create anything he could conceive. I never saw the trailer but heard tales that they still lived without air conditioning. As children, my brother and I had visited them for a week in another part of the Arizona desert. No air conditioning, in the heat of summer, I counted my minutes there as mere survival. On the day that Grandma died suddenly of a heart attack, Mom had left Indio, California to visit her folks. An easy drive of barely over 200 miles drive across the Sonoran Desert. Grandpa had been ill, and Mom intended to check on him.

The story goes that soon after Mom drove away, my dad got a call at work saying Grandma was dead. He was mortified that Mom, with no preparation, was heading toward a tragic throw of the dice. Grandpa was the one whose health was failing, not Grandma. Dad blasted the ten miles home, changed, and jumped into the Datsun 280Z sports car he had bought Mom as a gift. He put a custom DOT B license on the car to clearly delineate ownership, but we all know why he bought the car … right? He had the right car for what he did next. Interstate 10 is a divided four-lane freeway, seemingly going to nowhere until it crosses the Colorado River. He told us he rarely dropped the car below 100 MPH, blew by a highway patrol car hiding next to a freeway overpass, and even with Mom's hour head start he arrived only minutes after she did. He didn't want her to face the crushing news alone. My wife tells me that Blackwood men say I love you most clearly with their actions. Of course, we do.

Locked onto the east coast by my emerging panic disorder and inability to fly home, I wrote the first of several eulogies, this time mostly for the benefit of my mom. Reading the page now, I wonder how it landed. Clearly, the story of the wine bottles was not the only time I had perceived my grandmother as a victim of her domineering husband. My words also reflected the stridency of my youthful feminism. How else can explain beginning my memorial this way:

Her thoughts were of compassion and kindness. If she was possessed by an overriding tragic flaw it was her stubborn loyalty to the ideas and times that shaped her. Like a fragile bud that was never meant to expose its full beauty, she stood as a silent reminder of things that wouldn't be.

Wow, I was angry. As a child, I had seen Grandpa bully my grandmother. I paid less attention to him than I did her reactions. She had the hopeful eyes and automatic flinch of a dog that had been hit randomly but still sought affection and had given up trying to run away. Sometimes, the flinch was in her eyes, a reflexive narrowing; then she'd notice me and offer a gentle pursed smile. This reflex, this survival instinct is something I'd also seen in my mother, though, honestly, I don't think I ever put two and two together. A nervous child, I intuitively understood the body language of caution and self-protection. But the newly flaming second wave feminist me saw a cause bigger than my grandma:

The further I explore my memories of her, the more I realize the narrowness of her life. Certainly during her life she had shown the capacity to think, to manage, and to lead, but these inclinations were somehow suppressed. Like many of the women of her times, her life had begun as an example of quiet submission to the men around her. Her fruition as a human being could never and would never exceed her devotion to the man she married.

There was a message here to my mother. Mom was smart, something Dad always said about her. She was less his captive than a captive of the times. My mom was also the fruit of the bitter tree of her upbringing. She constantly underestimated herself even while providing proof of her capacity. Later, when we kids were gone, she succeeded in any career she tried, like gobbling up the classes to get her real estate broker license. But there was one refrain, a haunting memory of childhood that she told me often. She always wanted to learn to play the piano, but because her older sister didn't practice after her lessons, Mom wasn't allowed to try. Punished for her sister's failure, there would be no more money for her lessons. Mom always told me, wistfully, she never did learn to play the piano.

I was self-aware enough to realize my letter to my mom was a screed, but I sent it anyhow:

I see my bitterness and realize it is a condemnation of a system that separates many individuals from all the tantalizing possibilities they have within themselves.

I now know I was not only speaking for my grandma. I had recently been hit with the panic disorder that would derail my own possibilities and on behalf of my grandma Lois, I was also expressing my frustration. As Grandma was bullied, I felt bullied by my own mind and thoughts. But that understanding, my revelation of self, didn't come for decades.

Four months later, under the care of my mom, Grandpa Kerby died. We shared the same first name, James … Jim. Grandpa Kerby was a survivor. In the Second World War, he was a 'hump pilot' who flew supplies to the Nationalist Chinese from India over the Himalayan mountains. His plane was shot down over Japanese occupied China. Badly wounded, he was smuggled to safety through enemy lines. What he lacked in education, he made up for with a certain mechanical genius. He had fabricated farm implements still in use, but he was bitter that he had not patented any of his inventions. When we were kids, Jim and Lois occupied the big house on the ranch, a Spanish inspired mansion of sorts he had gained by managing the farm. It was a glorious child's playground. He doted on his grandkids, but even as a child, I sensed there was a hole in him he could never fill. He drove a big white Cadillac, owned a Bonanza private plane, entertained and drank wildly at the best restaurant in little Indio, and played endless rounds of golf at an exclusive desert course. Depression kid, not much education, WWII survivor, self-made man; in many ways he was a product of his times.

As my years moved into double digits, I recognized there were great differences between Grandpa and me. My status as a grandkid gave me a permission I don't think many people ever had with Grandpa. I could argue with him. I was in a Christian kid phase. He claimed to have no use for religion. He claimed his religion was nature, but I wanted him in a church. I was conscious of the social and political cauldron of the 60s. He was an arch conservative. In one argument, he revealed much about himself as we argued civil rights. He said, "I can't be a racist because my favorite entertainer was a one-eyed, n … Jew." I didn't understand who he was talking about until one of my relatives prompted, Sammy Davis Junior. Grandpa was proud of that claim. To be sure, he was carrying me because he enjoyed the fight. But I was far more interested in the world of adults than kids, so I loved those arguments. He would purposely goad me and bait me, but I didn't stop coming right back at him. I was conscious that during our debates he and I were in our own world. The other adults in the room backed away a step and watched. I wonder about that. Was I getting to do what they never could?

My mother's side of the family is renowned for the ability to create and hold dear a family grudge. Like the Blackwoods, the Kerby clan is Scots Irish, hill people who cherished the art of the feud. At one point, Grandpa, via neglect and mismanagement, was forced out of his position of ranch manager by my uncle, the husband of his oldest daughter. The hierarchy of the ranch was both physical and geographical. This meant that the son-in-law would be moving from a smaller house on the ranch, forcing his father-in-law out of the big house. This is Greek tragedy stuff. Power, family, anger, threats of violence, tears, the crash of a once great man. As a kid, it was all very confusing but one memory stuck.

In the living room of the great house was a memento of Grandad's service in the Second World War. On its tripod, perfectly preserved, was a Japanese water-cooled machine gun. The firing pin was removed and there was no ammunition, so it became a toy for all the male grandkids. This sort of trophy was common then. Hanging on the wall in my best friend's home, his dad had mounted a Japanese rifle he had brought home from the war. In the last act of my grandparents leaving the farm, my folks were there to load the trailer. Grandad said, "I only wish I had ammunition for that machine gun so I could put it in the back of the truck and shoot up this place on the way out." I remember looking at the old man and knowing ... knowing ... he was not kidding. The rest of his life he bore that grudge, and never spoke to his daughter again. When, decades later, my uncle and aunt visited my parents, they stayed out in the car while my cousin asked if it would be okay for them to come in and visit my mom. My dad intervened and told them to come in. The pain of that feud only ended when that generation all passed away.

When I got word of Grandpa Kerby's death, I realized I had set a precedent by writing about my grandmother. This one was going to be more of a struggle. I mused generally about death. I was stalling.

Death is all part of this constant process of life.

Good lord. The chutzpah. I had no idea what I was talking about. Our parents had sheltered us from death. I met and lost six of my great grandparents. In my mid-twenties, I had yet to go to a funeral.

Then I got to the heart of the matter:

For a wide variety of reasons, I have held a deep-seated disdain of my grandfather Kerby ... No developed social consciousness, a brutal need for authority, and intellectual insecurity plagued his life. For those things I understood and still oppose, I still speak ill of him.

Then the rest of the writing takes a turn. Even in the arrogance of my twenties, I knew when I was going too far. Oh, that didn't mean I paused to step back from my judgment. Awareness would not connect to action for some time to come. But now that I had vented to my grieving mother ... my grieving mother ... I had to write myself out of the corner. I knew I had to say something good, something uplifting. Looking at the words now, I see I decided to lie. It's a good lie, a plausible take on Grandpa, but this part was for Mom.

Childhood memories are either softened and embellished in the cleansing haze of time or heightened to clarity by repeated recollection.

Okay. I started with a disclaimer.

A part of myself that I cherish is my love and almost religious feeling toward the outdoors. This feeling was given to me, in great measure, by my grandfather. He often said that though he was not a religious man, he always had one cathedral that was the land, especially the mountain wilderness. I can remember that his mood would change while camping. His usually brash manner and words would yield to the scale of nature.

I went on to paint my grandpa as an environmentalist. Sure. Why not. Give him one of my values to paint a better picture for Mom. There was some recognizable truth in what I wrote. What I didn't write about was an afternoon camping in the White Mountains of Arizona and my grandpa teaching me how to use a rifle by tossing empty beer can after beer can into a rushing stream while we all blasted away at them from the bank, leaving the destroyed aluminum cans and all that lead to be a part of nature. But I did learn how to safely handle a .22 rifle.

I claimed his love of nature as mine. I think I wanted to let Mom know that there was a good legacy, too. In this, I think the memorial, brash and brutal though it was, was something my mother kept and cherished. I think I landed where she did in understanding her father's life. From the flaws, she, too, needed to find something good to hold, even if we had to make it up. I ended with a tortured sentence, a ham-handed attempt at solace.

In the end, it can only be hoped that all life's consciousness will become a contribution to continuance.

Yeah, he's in there somewhere, deep in my DNA. I relished, and still do, my slashing ability to argue a point. A little of the blue-collar chip that took permanent residence on my shoulder comes from the guy the system screwed over and never got those patents he deserved because he didn't know how to file the paperwork, and no one was there who could tell him how. My disdain for bullies was reinforced by watching my gentle and smart grandmother cower before one. I suppose that while my mom's parents are missing from the pages of my memoir, they are still there … everywhere.

STORIES

———————————

STORIES ARE OUR LIFETIME CURRENCY. They connect us. They help us remember. Miraculously, repeating a story over and over also helps us forget. Most people don't think of themselves as storytellers because the act of relating the events of the day are as natural as breathing.

Stories are also our collective memory. But time, like water, erodes and changes the memory landscape. Christians who stand by the literal interpretation of the Bible generally don't pause to consider the source of those stories. Nothing in the New Testament was written down until almost 100 years after the death of Jesus. The text is a 100-year-old game of telephone. Ever play that game? A sentence cannot make its way around from speaker to listener without changing. Now imagine that game going on for 100 years. Buddhist texts existed for over 500 years before they were first written down. Traditions under the umbrella of Buddhism were turned into long chants. Those chants change by region and dialect. The Old Testament was an oral tradition handed over to scribes. In the ancient world, fidelity to the transmitted word wasn't a consideration. Scribes had preferences and opinions that they added across the centuries. A couple of scholarly nuns taught me how to slice the Old Testament apart to reveal different schools of scribes. All writers, like gamblers, have tells.

An enormous part of the world believes they have found a solution to the problem of holy provenance. Islamic tradition holds as its core tenant that the stories of the Koran were transmitted to Mohammad by an angel and then immediately written down. The Koran is assumed to be the definitive word of God because it was never a wandering oral tradition first. I wonder. Under that criteria, would not the more recently written texts of Mormonism, as transmitted by another angel to Joseph Smith, actually be the one true path because they are God's most recent amendments? Mormons think so.

I come from a family tradition of storytelling. Only later did I discover that this was not the case with all families. I am not sure why I fell so easily into the role of rapt listener, but I understood early on that my favorite books began, "Once upon a time …" and when someone in my family said, "I remember …" it was the same thing. I found the attempt to find resonance with other human beings via the story enthralling, if not an ecstatic. Maybe that is why I also felt an obligation to maintain the stories and eventually keep them alive by writing them down. The first scribe to record an oral tradition must have felt the same compulsion.

I recall my early fascination with words beginning with the discovery that in my thin, colorfully illustrated children's books there was a relationship between the pictures and the words. At first, the words were the voice of my mother. I don't think I ever heard my dad read a story. When I could read, the words became my own voice. Quickly it was the words, not the pictures, that held me spellbound. I soon wanted books with more words because I discovered with the words alone, I could paint my own pictures, illustrate my own inner books. I skipped comic books, almost completely—too many pictures. My superheroes were the mysterious, distant people who wrote the words. Nowhere around me was anyone whom I could identify as a writer. The isolation of my small town and the distance to the people who wrote the books made the writers more mysterious. By the time puberty struck, I was already wondering how I could be one of those distant people: the writers.

Writers don't need readers as much as they need to write. With practice and diligence, someone can learn to be a good written communicator. That is an important skill. But when I think of a writer, I am referring to someone compelled to memorialize life, whose very mental balance is linked to being able to get things out of her head and on the page.

I have a garbage bin brain. Random stuff gets tossed in by passersby and accumulates. After a while, the detritus under its own weight gets compressed and stinks. Push the garbage down. Create space. The sloughed off remains keep coming. Then it's full. The accumulation continues, more nasty bits are carefully mounded on top. That's a losing game because pieces start falling on the ground around the bin. You've seen the cans on the street. Now it seems like it's reasonable to surround the full bin with more garbage. Toss the crap close by and call it good.

A writer, the compelled storyteller, feels the bin filling up. Little tingles of emotion come and go as it fills. *Oh, that's interesting. No, I didn't really need to know that. Why did I waste time reading that guy? That thought makes me happy. More, please. Why do I feel depressed? Where did that come from? Who did this to me?* Day after day, the writer sifts and sorts the accumulating flotsam. There is no way to stop the fretting and judging. And then it happens; with no other place to go, the writer starts dumping his accumulated garbage on the people around him. In my case, out comes the sullenness, sarcasm, anger, or the endless bad jokes. It's time. The writing begins.

A journal. An observed scene on a napkin at a bar. An idea tapped out on the phone. A short story. A letter to the editor. An essay spewed out to the internet. A book. There is no stopping once the damn bursts. Pages that will never be seen by another soul fill notebooks. I feel better. Order is restored. The garbage disappears from the street, the sidewalk, the bin. All those random pieces now have a home on the page or in the computer file. They are not so much free as merely contained someplace else, which was always the point. The curse is that everything seems important enough to record.

In politics, there is a moment before a vote where the elected official 'creates a record.' To the outside observer, those little speeches are seen as self-serving and gratuitous. On some level that's true. But most importantly, creating a record is an explanation for all history of why the official chose to vote the way he or she did. That record becomes the answer for every subsequent question.

As a writer, I am always creating a record. Beyond my own catharsis, I don't underestimate the patina of narcissism that gradually covers this endeavor. What sane person thinks that every thought has value? I make no claim for sanity. The writing is mostly an attempt to create stability, a state adjacent to sanity. The feedback loop of a growing stack of random writing is like a ballast on a ship, stones below the waterline, mostly invisible but essential to keep the ship right side up.

I suppose it is inevitable that there comes a moment when I admit that what I really want is a reader. The storyteller, the keeper of the knowledge, is little more than a strange, obsessive neurotic if there is no way to tell the story to someone else. At various points, while writing journal entries, I have thought about who might read them. I wondered if someone would be curious about what I thought or, with my passing, all those words would end up on an anonymous stack on its way to the dump. If you have lived a death, you have seen what happens to those things once deemed precious by the departed. The objects, forever deprived of context and meaning layered on them by the owner, become a curious burden to be disposed of by family and friends. I have a drawer of such bequeathed items. Certainly, some bits find a new home as a reminder of times past, moments shared, but mostly, for the great sort at the end of a life, there is too much to consider, too many waves of emotion to spend much time bouncing from touchstone to touchstone. Caught in the grief fatigue, with a little pang of regret, the pieces that are finally too much are thrown away … and lost forever.

In my neighborhood, the streets fill with cars when estate sale signs pop up on street corners. There is a gold rush spirit to the early arrivers who are looking for the hidden gem among the tables and tables of … well … stuff. I have roamed into an estate sale or two but have never bought a thing. Mostly, I see ghosts. Who was this person? Did someone die in one of these rooms? How many Thanksgiving dinners were served on those neatly stacks dishes, each with its own hand scribbled price tag? I can't do what many folks find easy. I can't separate the items from the previous owners, especially when that item has lived for many years in the place where it is being sold. I wonder which pieces had a special meaning that will now forever be unknown.

Since I was a child, I have been plagued by a vision of books on shelves. On my little black and white TV, I once saw a tour of the Library of Congress. I was consumed with the idea that Thomas Jefferson's personal library was the seed corn of that wonderful place. Near the end of the show, amidst the vastness of the library, the presenter walked up to a single collection of books on shelves. It didn't seem like a lot of books to me but as he slowly backed up along the wall, he said that this was the number of books an average person would read in a lifetime. *My God!* I thought. *That really isn't so many books. That's all we get? But there are so many books.* Whenever I pick up a book, the mental picture of that wall returns to plague me. Choose wisely, mister, you don't get so many of these.

That is why the books at estate sales catch me up short. You can read people by what they read. More importantly, if they were readers, the books you see are almost never all the books they ever owned. What has remained on the shelves is the result of years of culling, a carefully curated library that had special meaning to the owner. I know the categories because I am that person. There are books that came as gifts, possibly inscribed. It is entirely likely that those books do not reflect the taste of the owner; rather, they are kept as a reminder that there once was someone kind enough to try to find a book that the owner may like. Those books are symbols of the giver. Books are kept as reminders to the owners of their life, the evolution of their tastes and thinking over time. Seemingly random on the shelf, they are a timeline known only to one. If someone knew the owner looks closely, he would be confused by books that didn't reflect the person he thought he knew. We mostly get to know people as slices of their life. Origins remain a mystery. More intriguing still are the books kept only to remind one of emotions the owner once felt at the precise moment she read the book for the first time. We cannot know the number of times the reader pulled those books down and read a few pages to conjure up joy or melancholy or even lust. No aura surrounds the musty pages that can tell us the power of a single tome. Finally, there are books that show their age. Sometimes these members of the library have seemingly random book markers, torn bits of paper or a marker from a long-departed bookstore, popping out from the pages. Was this where the owner stopped reading and never returned, or does the softness of the pages, the friction tears at the corners, the scribble in the margins reveal that these books were companions, the ones returned to many times to repeat a lesson, encourage a smile, or bolster fading memory. These select few are not so much books as old friends.

If the person was an unpublished writer, then something is missing from the stacks of books: their words. All those hours, pen or pencil in hand, pounding typewriter keys, tapping away at keyboards are treated as if they have no value. No little price tag stuck in a corner can resurrect them. They are merely the musings of a stranger. I have looked, poked around, and have never seen a journal laid out among the offered collections. Those pages, a few read with some curiosity, will disappear back into a box in the dark, too precious to immediately disappear, but disappear they will.

This seems a sad, inevitable fate for a lifetime effort. The writer without a reader. But that's the thing about being a storyteller compelled to write one's thoughts down somewhere. Ultimately, it remains the truly singular act of finding one's self. Plagued with an excess of introspection, the act of writing is a joyful release of the growling goblins and spinning muses. Longing to be read remains longing. But longing to write and tell one's stories has a cure. It is an act both simple and endlessly complex, this spreading of one's soul and mind on a page. It is the storyteller's obligation. In the end, it is the essence of happy necessity. And that will have to do.

SAND

————————

SAND GETS EVERYWHERE. Try to stop it. It will find the crack in a wall, wrap around the edge of the slightly ajar window, and collect in a sweaty fold of skin. After a day in the dunes, the first blast of water in a hot shower will leave rivulets of sand at your feet. A whisk broom on the front porch will pile most of the sand in a corner but leave a silky layer of the grit behind. Heat defined the air in my desert, but it was the sand I loved. In the midday sun, the white, crusty surface was hot in bare feet, but the more I wiggled my toes and scuffled my feet the secret cool below welcomed me. I lay back on the form fitting sand in the shade and felt the chill wrap around my body. I would stroke my hands across the surface in wide arches and feel the abrasive tingling massage. In my little boy world, sand was a playmate.

Desert towns march out into the sand, conquering it one row of low ranch style homes block by block. Before the next row of houses appeared behind my childhood home, the sand was but a few steps from our back door. It accumulated in the wind shadow of tumble weeds or on the lee side of any object. The wind blew consistently down from the mountain passes creating narrowing fingers of white sand all reaching the same direction. For any child, sand was an invitation. *Come, step on me, let me wrap around your feet. Sift me through your fingers. Throw me in the air and watch me disappear in the breeze. Build forts, push toy cars, and the next time you come here, after the wind does it work, I will be right back the way you found me, waiting for you to start again.*

The Coachella Valley, at the bottom of California, is a special kind of desert. All deserts are arid, crusty, and defined by the scarcity of water. The plants, nature's tough guys, built to suck up brief showers, grow in a sprint, then stand resolute in the moisture hunting sunshine. Cacti are inverted water wells, storing above ground what can't be found in the soil below. The creatures, sunshine escape artists, hunt in the evening chill, leaving ghost trails in the sand visible with the rising sun. Dragged lizard tails, the sideway Ss of rattlesnakes and delicate spread toe stamps of road runner claws. But be careful in the midday sun. Look closely. Step precisely. The shade of rock outcrops or stubborn plants are cool beds where a sleeping rattlesnake may be enjoying a daytime siesta.

To live in a desert is to cultivate special eyes. What a stranger might call desolate or hostile, I called home. Even now, I feel my body relax when the view in front of me browns and opens up to the horizon. The elbows and ribs of the resting body of surrounding mountains touch the valley as foothills. In its openness, the desert hides nothing and everything. That is the great illusion. Its emptiness is full.

The vast, brown desert looks tough. It's a lie. Look closely. You will see the tracks of countless vehicles, permanent marks on the desert floor. Once broken, the soil's crust will stay scarred and vulnerable for hundreds of years. When it finally arrives, rain will seek out the man-made cracks and use them as paths for new erosion. Before the World War II American Army made its way to the Northern Africa desert to face the Desert Fox, Rommel, they came to a part of my desert to train. Climb the right hills, look across the landscape, and ghostly imprints of tank tracks are still visible.

For a geologic instant, a small part of my desert was unique.

Miles and miles of great rolling dunes covered our valley floor. In the soft, white sand, human steps and tracks would be erased by every windstorm. Launched by the wind, when the sand came back to earth, the dunes were once again pristine. To drive from my home in Indio to Palm Springs, twenty miles, I headed out into those dunes. Past the city limits, after feeling the jolt of gravity in my gut in the rise and fall through the high, storm-catching dikes, I emerged into the dunes. The straight, two-lane road teased me to take a speed run through the one stop sign for eight miles at a crossroads. At night, other headlights visible for miles, it seemed safe. Foot on the gas, I reached down to flip off my headlights and float though the intersection … invisible … immortal. (The immorality of a teenager with a car.)

If you look around the dunes and hills very closely, you can see signs of water everywhere. Desert rain is most often a violent outburst. Parched though the land may be, it can only stand a sip of water at a time. Quickly sated, water is then left to gravity and its own will. Down, ever down in growing flash flood torrents until it finds the lowest resting place, the rolling brown water then quickly disappears. Streambeds, arroyos, frozen in the time of the last deluge slice the landscape. Eluvial fans of rock and soil reach out in ever widening tumbles from every canyon, bringing the mountain bit by bit out onto the desert floor. Rocks and boulders, of all sizes, litter the fan, each remnant softened and rounded by the spasmodic tumbling down the hills in thousands of years of momentary, roiling cascades.

The Valley, that's what we call it, has a geology guaranteed to swat away ego. On the west side a sharp, young mountain range rises to the dominant peak of Mt. San Jacinto standing over 10,000 feet tall. I could stand sweating in 110-degree heat and look up at snow. Lower cousins of the great peak make a U-shape embrace of the valley looking out toward the Salton Sink hundreds of feet below sea level. A geologic dance between the Colorado River and one of the earth's great depressions; water and sun has created and evaporated several generations of long-lost lakes. The current brackish lake, the Salton Sea, is a man-made mistake. A canal dike holding cold Colorado River water gave way. The futility of man and water. The Sink filled for over a year. For a time, dreamers came to the Salton Sea, brought great saltwater sport fish, docks, and pushed land into speculative tracts for new resorts. But the sea became deadly, fish died, and the dreamers fell away to find new dreams. That now deadly sea would have disappeared long ago except for the toxic fertilizer-rich runoff of hundreds of farms. Water and gravity, the old conspirators.

Both the fertility of the valley and all that sand are a gift from the Colorado River. About a thousand years ago, the

Colorado River damned by its own silt, stopped flowing into the Gulf of California and instead rushed into my valley. For several hundred years, an enormous fresh-water lake, fed by the river, defied the natural evaporation process, filling the valley right up into the foothills. Look up forty feet or more at the rocky edge of mountains and you will see the travertine rock that marks the shoreline of that ancient lake. Look again, a few feet below, and you will see 400-year old rows of huge bowls of stacked rocks built by the Cahuilla Indians as fish traps. Sifting the silt at the bottom of the dunes, my child's hands found what we called seashells and if we were very lucky, Indian arrowheads. We believed all that sand came from the ocean because no one ever told us about the giant freshwater lake.

About the time Spanish explorers came to the valley the lake disappeared. The capricious Colorado River reopened its path to the gulf, draining the land and letting the sun finish the job of expunging the lake. The river silt became the agricultural loam of the Imperial and Coachella valleys. The sand? That became our magnificent child's sandbox.

I don't recall anyone ever saying we were about to have a 'windstorm.' We called them sandstorms. On the eastern hip of Mt. San Jacinto is a pass between two mountain ranges. It is how you leave the valley on your way to Los Angeles and it is there, on the downslope, the wind originates. The wind is so reliable that the pass is now littered with thousands of windmills, part of the iconography of the city of Palm Springs seen in a dozen movies.

When the sandstorms boiled up, the sky in the direction of the pass became brown with sand, two kinds of sand. The light, silty sand flew up hundreds of feet into the sky. The heavier, gritty sand rarely blew higher than an adult's head, stinging eyes and scraping a face. The day after a storm its severity could be measured in two ways. First, by how much sand was on our front porch and back patio. My job was to sweep and shovel away the latest deposit from the desert. Before I started sweeping, I liked to look at the ripples of miniature dunes on our front porch, as pristine as the big dunes nearby. This is the sand that had eyes for the slightest crack or opening. It invited itself in, giving the slightest sensation of grit under bare feet in the kitchen. I learned never to wipe off a car after a sandstorm. Touch the car and you scratch it. A blast from the hose was the only way to safely remove that sand.

Second was the low sand: the destroyer. It manifested as sandblasted, slightly gobbled fence posts and house siding for those who lived closest to the dunes. But for a car crazy family, owners of two service stations, we would see the damage on the cars of those unlucky, or dumb enough, to drive out into the sandstorm. If they had been on the freeway, you could tell the way they were headed by which side of the car was dulled and missing paint. Windshields, headlights, chrome, and plastic were all pocked and abraded by the low sand. All would have to be replaced. For locals, driving in a sandstorm had to be an essential trip. It was too expensive to get caught out in a sandstorm for no good reason.

As adolescents, most of my buddies and I had motorcycles. We often headed out into the dunes. Once up to speed, a motorcycle glides across the top of white sand dunes. The knowledge that the sand would grant us a soft landing only encouraged recklessness. If you lost control, the trick was to jump away from the motorcycle and pray it didn't follow you to where you landed. That worked, most of the time. There were casualties, but the bumps and casts made for good stories later. There is one thing everyone did once and never again. Cascading down the highest dunes was the greatest temptation. At the base was a wind eddy where fine silt accumulated. Except for a slight black tint, a sparkling in the right sunlight, it didn't look much different than the rest of the dune. But on the downhill run, the silt could suddenly swallow the front wheel of your motorcycle. Launched over the bike, headfirst, not breaking your neck was the goal. You only had to learn that lesson once.

With helmets, goggles, and a bandana tied across our faces, we sometimes braved the blowing sand and headed out into sandstorms. Stopping on top of a dune, engines off, we heard and felt the desert. Any exposed skin was victim to a thousand little bites as the sand hit and wrapped around us. In a gust, the sensation was unpleasant enough to flinch and turn away. Even inside the helmet, the desert was telling us to be quiet. Shhhhhhh, it said, as the rivulets of sand wrapped around our feet and tires. We tried to ride with the wind at our backs. Two showers later, sand still showed up in the bottom of the tub.

Once I had my own car, I had access to the secret, and not-so-secret, places where bored desert kids would come to drink beer, do drugs, listen to loud music, and for a fortunate few, get laid. One such place was called, appropriately, Jamaica Sands. In the 50s and 60s land speculators and grifters bought chunks of cheap desert sand, put in utilities and carved out asphalt roads and curbed cul-de-sacs. Usually, somewhere near the presumed entrance, was an optimistic billboard proclaiming a future community. Mostly, the communities didn't happen. Eventually the sign, faded and sand blasted, blew down and the roads were buried by the creeping tentacles of sand dunes. For industrious partiers, these abandoned sites were perfect. All we had to do was coax our car or truck over the creeping dune fingers to the bare pavement in the middle of the ghost developments. Inside our hormone-enveloped forts, we were free of adult supervision. Kegs were hauled in, trunks full of beer were opened, joints lit, and eight-track music cranked up. Best of all, on moonlit nights, the light reflecting off the white dunes erased the night enough to play pick-up football games in the sand.

Everyone knew the configuration of the front lights of the Sherriff's Plymouth. While we could spot them in the distance, we weren't fooling them. A generation before they were the ones playing in the dunes. Sometimes they blockaded the way into the party. Gallons of beer poured into those same dunes; we were told to go home. Bottlenecked leaving our hiding place, drunk drivers were scooped up on the way out. More than once, we were pulled over by the deputies to push a stuck car out of sand so that it could be towed, and its driver taken away.

There was a time when the desert mostly attracted the dreamers and the desperate. For years, speeding out from my home on the Interstate 10, I looked out across broad stretches of the desert and saw small homesteader cabins. Sand stacked up against the windward side, wood siding and roofs blown off, roads to them but faint outlines, I always wondered who thought moving there was a good idea. What strange need for space drove them? Gradually, they eroded away on the wind. But not all of them. There were a couple of survivors, maybe driven by an immeasurable stubbornness or an overwhelming desire to be alone; little green islands in the distance, they clung to those vast tracks of their desert land.

The single highlight of my miserable year at a junior college in the desert was a geology class. The class used two big, white four-wheel drive International Harvester Travelalls driven by graduate students. It turned out that, while a native, I didn't know anything about the desert. We stopped in front of an imposing 200-foot face of sand, gravel, and enormous boulders. *More foothills*, I thought. No, the Martinez Slide. One day, before humans came to the Valley, the top of a mountain fell and didn't stop until its momentum died on the desert floor. *A mountain can just fall down?* I thought. I had been in a few earthquakes and vaguely knew the San Andreas Fault was nearby. I didn't know the foothills behind my house, my motorcycle playground, was the actual crack in the earth. I'd camped among the palm trees. Smoked joints and looked down at the lights of Indio. We stopped the Travelalls where seeping spring water kept the soil moist.

The professor handed me a shovel and said, "Want to see the fault?"

"But isn't that where we are?" I asked.

"No, the actual fault."

I dug where he pointed. A few feet down, I hit a layer of small rocks.

"You found it," he said.

At the point where the tectonic plates meet, the pressure grinds the rocks into a small tight layer. It's the geological water barricade that forces the water table to the surface, feeding the palms. I let a handful of rocks fall between my fingers and never looked at that squat range of brown hills the same again.

The world of sand I knew is an old man's fable now. The valley is now the home of over 100 golf courses surrounded by condos and homes on neatly cared-for streets. The majority of these communities are fenced off. You only see inside them if your name is left with the guard at the gate. The rolling dunes have been plowed, leveled, and simply disappeared into an air conditioned, sprinklered, momentarily green world that could be anywhere. Truth is, it should be anywhere but a desert.

I didn't fly home to my desert for almost twenty years. I had told my wife endless tales of what it was like there and on our first trip I set out to show her the sand. I drove and drove but could not find the dunes. Finally, at the very edge of Indio, I found a small plot that had not been developed. It was at the place where we used to cross over the giant flashflood preventing dikes. Crossing over was no longer possible as that road was now an artificial lake in the middle of yet another gated country club. I walked out and she took pictures of me standing on a sad little sand ridge in the lee side of a tumble weed, a pathetic remnant of my childhood.

Inevitably, a piece of the desert has now been preserved as a park. It felt familiar. I even told Sally not to get too comfortable in the shade of a rock lest a rattler emerge. But the big dunes were gone. There was no place to struggle to the top of a dune, then slide down the other side on our butts. We walked neat paths, with signs warning us to 'Stay on the Path.' I felt the slight resonance of home, but not the old, expansive shout of joy. My dunes were now reduced to a roadside attraction.

"Well," I said to my wife, "It used to be kind of like this."

Driving away, I took solace in two things. If you live in a desert, you must do so with some humility. The desert always wins. What humans build there depends on water and water in the desert is a demon spirit weaving the illusion that it will always be available. Then there is the shadow. Climb up the right hill just before the sun begins to set behind the looming Mt. San Jacinto, and on a clear day you can see the shadow of the mountain reach out from the mountain's base and slowly work its way across the desert. As the shadow comes to wherever you are standing in the desert, you can relax your eyes, let go of the protective squint, and feel the temperature drop a few degrees. As night falls, you can close your eyes and still see sand dunes.

CAMERA

I FULLY EMBRACE the melancholy of nostalgia. Some people are strident. Never look back. There may be some truth to the idea that we are better people if we stay in the moment or are optimistic about the future. I can do a little of both, but I am constantly drawn to the past, especially the physical past all around me. I live in a city that has been 'hot' for some time now. Hotness attracts waves of newcomers. Hotness rejects nostalgia. Hotness is almost entirely forward looking. And hotness consumes the past in giant gulps, barely pausing to chew and digest before reaching for the next tasty morsel. There is no place where hotness is more real in a big city than the streetscape and skyline.

Since I arrived in Portland over three decades ago, there is a little game I play with myself that I call, "What was there?" As buildings come down and open spaces fill up, I try to remember what was there before; more than remember, I stare at the new until I can conjure up a picture of the old. On one corner downtown, I stand in a park and look at the street corners across the street. Now they contain a high-rise hotel, coffee shop, restaurant, and huge federal courthouse. In my mind, the hotel becomes a three-story brick building that housed my favorite downtown dive bar. The courthouse turns into the low-slung building where I stuffed envelopes for the Gary Hart presidential campaign. On that block were three- and four-story brick and wood buildings that housed a non-profit providing homelessness services, a dry cleaner, a reggae club, and a Chinese restaurant.

In my own neighborhood, I grab a slice of pizza, look out the window of the parlor and see another dive bar, open early for the alcoholics' first drink of the day and a barbershop where now stands a Starbucks. Down the street a row of tall, muscular condominiums stands in the ghost of an Arby's and a parking lot where I could always find a place for my car while running errands. When I arrived on the block there were six used bookstores for different tastes: Marxist tomes at the Jack Reed and mysteries at Murder by the Book, the wonderfully musty aroma of aging tomes at Beaver Books. Now there are two Powell's bookstores, one in a former Chinese/American restaurant where the elders of the family were always sitting, smoking at one big round table in the back, latest copies of Chinese language newspapers in their hands. The game goes on and on. I can't stop it, this job of secret street historian. But now the change has escalated to a point that exceeds my memory. I get lost driving in parts of the city because my deeply imprinted landmarks have been erased and replaced. This is becoming a problem, my strange problem.

At the junction of this problem there is yet another conundrum. It's what I am doing right now, sitting at my computer, hands on a keyboard, looking inward to see what emerges on the screen in front of me. I write. I write a lot. Like my little memory game, I love the writing. Both passions connect me to myself on a spectrum of emotions. The life of an essayist is a little noble and a lot therapeutic. But always, no matter the catalyst, I end up looking inward … inward … inward.

One day, sitting any my computer and staring out the window to see what words were floating by, it occurred to me that I was dangerously out of balance. All this inward eyeballing was going to become a problem. I went for a walk. While walking I saw yet another temporary chain-link fence erected around a 100-year-old house that was not long for this world. My need to load my memory with the old house suddenly felt like a burden, not a fun little mind game, an overwhelming obligation if not an obsession. Happy melancholy was happy no more.

Over the years, I had used everyone's ubiquitous camera, my iPhone, to take pictures of places about to go missing, but I was never consistent about it. Not part of the selfie generation, I sometimes forget I have a camera in my pocket at all. I have owned a series of cameras that were only slightly more than a phone. A little better resolution, a bit longer reach, but really, not worth the effort. On a vacation to San Diego, I saw my niece use what seemed like a pretty nice camera as she escorted us around the zoo. More than the pictures themselves, I was taken by her relationship with her camera. I saw her think about her shots, twiddle with knobs, click, reconsider, then repeat until she was satisfied. *What was she really doing,* I thought? But more than the process, I loved the little moments of solitude she created while taking the pictures. The crowds around her disappeared as she became absorbed in her subject. It seemed like a meditation, a place intimate and apart but vitally connected. When not shooting, she was very much attuned to the world around her, the light, the shadows, the potential subjects. There was clearly a hierarchy of needs she was pursuing to make photos that connected her to the world.

Those observations came back to me when I thought about how I had lost a sense of balance while perpetually caught in the feedback loop with my computer screen. I considered what it would be like to be a guy with a camera. You know those guys and girls, they never seem to be without a camera slung over their shoulder. Yeah, I looked at them, too, and judged, 'camera geek.' What a pain in the ass it must be to always carry that camera. Isn't their phone enough?

Now, the fun part. I knew absolutely nothing about cameras. Nothing. The happy side of my 'I don't know' place is the headlong pursuit of knowing. I got books at the library. I chatted with my niece. I bought books. And, god help me, I fell into the abyss that is YouTube. Up until this point, I had used YouTube mostly looking for ways to fix things. Plumbing, electrical wiring, cars and gardens, there is someone somewhere who has taken it upon himself or herself to teach. It's strange to think there are people who feel the need to record themselves replacing the wax ring under an American Standard toilet but there they are, utterly serious, and with not a lick of self-consciousness. Lord knows, these caring strangers have saved my ass more than once, buying back hours of frustration and dead ends doing things I might have figured out on my own ... or not. Now I turned to these same earnest strangers to tell me about cameras. I discovered people whose livelihood seems to be making one video after another about everything to do with photography and others who seemed earnest but hopeless. At times, the people were more fascinating than anything they were saying about cameras.

YouTube grabbed me by the throat. I was watching videos day and night. I suddenly had favorite YouTubers. This process of trusting strangers on screens is a little scary. Humans sift other humans into boxes, starting with friend or foe. As I watched these strangers, I was suddenly an expert on what photography advise I could trust. Foolhardy confidence. The exercise becomes one of learning how I trust strangers. Did they seem sincere and knowledgeable? Did they care about the production aspects of their video? Were they friendly, someone I would like to talk to in the real world? Did they talk down to me or did they respect the fact that I was clueless? Basically, I was sorting for the traits of a talented con man.

I immersed myself in the endless comparison reviews on camera geek sites. This has long been one of my best things. Before the internet existed, I subscribed to *Consumer Reports* magazine. Few things excite me like comparative reviews with their rows of features and columns of red dots and empty circles. I have spent hundreds of hours reading reviews for products I never wanted, and would never buy, just to see which one somebody thought was the best. And once a year … oh my … the rapture of the appearance of the annual car buying guide. That little paperback was given a place of honor next to the toilet providing months and months of reading during an essential activity.

I was narrowing in. I discovered that I could spend thousands of dollars on this new obsession but that would never do. I have a lifelong habit of starting a hobby, mastering its essentials, then abandoning it once I 'figure it out.' (Anyone need a full set of beer making gear?) I found that what had happened to cameras while I ignored them was second nature to me. I love gadgets. Cameras had become computers that my new YouTube friends told me only a few could ever master. I learned the difference between a camera body and the lens. The interchangeable combinations seemed endless. When you had the camera and lens, the world opened up to an avalanche of camera gear. Why hadn't anyone told me about this before? I love figuring stuff out and tinkering. I love gear. How had I missed this?

The most dangerous moment came. The research ended. Fantasy became reality. We have all done it, pursued that thing, that place, that person, only to feel your innards turn to sludge when you have what you wanted so badly. Sometimes, so vested in the process, we cling to the dream as long as we can, if only to save face, having made a fool of ourselves by bragging to others about our quest. If we are lucky, the object of desire holds some continuing warmth. But as often as not, goodbyes are said and rationalizations are made. This very human reality is the reason basement shelves, garage rafters and the backs of drawers were invented. I became a camera owner.

This time seems different. (Hey, I'm not rationalizing yet. You hear me! Not rationalizing!) Maybe it was the nature of my intent. I have an ongoing need to be in balance, looking inward and outward. The complexity of the new device is not something that will be easily resolved. When I master the baby steps there is still a daunting mountain to climb. I stick with things I never figure out … like writing.

Through the little screen or viewfinder, I have discovered that I have accidentally created new eyes. The world around me is now not so defined by the name and nature of each object as a collection of component pieces. Color, shadow, light … oh my … light. I had no idea. I now find myself looking at the quality of the light and wondering what the corner of an interesting building would look like on a cloudy day, under bright sunshine, or the slanted rays of a fading winter day with shadows lengthening. I have experienced that little world apart that I saw my niece enter. A world where tiny adjustments to knobs, the rotation of the earth, and a step right or left completely alters an image. A world where it is impossible to exhaust the nature of one place.

I now have a little project to take me outdoors. The surest sign that history is about to be ground away is the appearance of two things: graffiti and a temporary cyclone fence around a building. The deals have been done and the building is a now an asset to be consumed and regurgitated as something else. Like those nerdy kids I used to scorn in high school, I now travel with my camera. Walking or driving, I take the time to stop and photograph all those slices in time that I have been trying to keep in my head. I try to see the details that will soon be lost in those places that were once so important to someone. Somebody lived there. Somebody worked there. As I shoot, I imagine what that place would have looked like in its prime, maybe the first day the happy souls walked in the front door. I take many shots through the fence, leaving a galvanized silver halo around my subject. There is a futility to this project. Like much of my writing, few will consume the final product. Most won't care I have taken the time at all. In the end, it's the melancholy of it all I seek. And maybe a momentary conquest of the momentum of life.

Now I know what to do when the words dry up, when

my mind and heart are momentarily exhausted. I take my camera and set out in any direction, gauging the light, looking for a shot. I cut the chain to the inward focused anchor and look away until I feel my feet set firmly on the ground again, weight balanced, eyes searching.

MUSIC

––––––––––––––––––

ONE OF THE FIRST INDEPENDENT ACTS for children is their choice of music. Of course, the first notes are provided for them by their parents, but discernment happens early. By a mysterious sorting, akin to the turned-up nose or voracious bite to proffered food, children decide what music they like. Inevitably, mind-numbingly to all around them, they will demand that music repeat ad nauseum. As a small child, I was gifted a small case that opened up to be a turntable with a single awful speaker. Secreted away in my room, I played records I had begged my parents to buy … over and over and over. This was the beginning of a soundtrack for my life that will only end when I do.

There were only two AM rock and roll radio stations in the valley. Well, there were kind of two. The one in Indio was purely pop rock, but the station in Palm Springs, which we could only get at night, seemed to favor a little harder rock. In retrospect, I think the only real difference was that the Palm Springs station had a slightly longer playlist, so the songs didn't repeat as often. In my room, or in the car there was rarely a moment when I didn't have the radio on in the background. I had a keen ear for when a new song, or new artist, plopped into the on-air rotation. Not understanding that music was a business, I was mystified why some songs seemed to disappear.

Music was dear. I mowed lawns or cleaned windows at Grandpa's service station, so I had my own spending money. No allowances. Dad said our allowance was a roof over our head and three meals a day. Fair enough. Oh, and no paying for grades. Getting a good report card was our job.

When it came to albums, the magic number was three ... three bucks ... a huge amount of money. In a time when most people curate their music one song at a time, it's difficult to understand the importance of an album. For an almost teenager who was developing a little edge in music choices, AM radio was mostly a wasteland. FM radio with its more obscure rock bands and long play sets was on the horizon, figuratively and literally. The idea of free form underground FM radio was beginning to take hold and when it did appear, we only got it from San Diego at night by rigging up elaborate cobwebs of wire in our rooms to make a more sensitive antenna. I read about bands in our link to the outside world—*Rolling Stone*—and had maybe only heard one popular song from an album before I put down my three dollars to hear an entire album.

Sliding my thumbnail along the album edge to cut open the plastic shrink wrap was an occasion most often done with friends. All senses were alive. The smell of the new vinyl. The pictures and words on an album sleeve, the liner notes within. The sheen of the pristine black disk before it had fingerprints or scratches. The music we were about to hear would never sound better than the first time we played it. We were entering the uncharted territory of album deep cuts, the songs that never played on the radio. The shock and joy of what we heard registered on our faces. Part of the fun was seeing how our friends reacted as we heard the songs together for the first time. If a song was a banger, we jumped and punched the air. When the music didn't excite, it was a crushing disappointment. Damn. Three dollars wasted.

We learned that the sequence of songs was not an accident. Bands chose how they to revealed albums to us. Mood, speed, tone, counter programming one song against the next one. Part of the joy was listening to record sides was speculating on the band's intent. Loyalties were formed to sides of albums. Long arguments ensued. Whoever put the record on got to choose the side. Sometimes there was absolute agreement that one could never play sides out of the original sequence because that would violate the nature of the album. Door closed, music turned up loud, we began to create our own sonic universe. Our parents mostly hated our albums and that was often the point as we began the slow, study work of carving out adulthood.

Lives have pivot points. Sometimes those moments wrap around success or failure. Perhaps the frozen moment you meet your first great love. Sometimes, there is an intimate death that shakes you to your core. For many parents, it is the first cry of their newborn. Look up from this page and I bet you can catalogue those rare moments in your life. Awash in music, I know the precise moment it changed me, an epiphany I have sought to repeat across my years.

Indio was impossibly far away from anything cool. One day, listening to the local AM radio station, my music buddy Greg and I screamed out loud in our screechy twelve-year-old voices when we heard the DJ say, "Something big is coming to Indio and our clue is 'light and heavy.'" We knew instantly that Iron Butterfly was coming. Greg, with a little more money in his family, had a bigger record collection and a better stereo but I had the Iron Butterfly album. Heavy metal rock was becoming a thing and in 1968 nothing was heavier than the over seventeen minutes of In-A-Gadda-Da-Vida with its rambling guitar jam and lyrics that made no earthly sense. The fact we even knew that song made us special because in the three-minute song confines of AM radio the only way you knew the song at all was to pony up the three bucks for the album. Greg and I played it endlessly.

Iron Butterfly was going to play at the Riverside County Fairgrounds, home of the mid-winter (winter is not at thing in the desert) Indio Date Festival. If you grew up in the desert early independence was to be handed two bucks, a small chuck of time, an assigned meeting place, and then being set free to run wild at the Date Festival. For the 4H kids that meant the animal displays. We ignored the displays of rocks and pies and went right to the carnival with its rides and sharp-eyed barkers looking to weasel away our bounty one dime at a time. Now, *our* band was coming, improbably, to the same arena where we watched the camel races and took elephant rides. Greg and I had to convince our parents to let us go to our first rock show. Maybe the fairgrounds seemed safe to them, maybe it was time for one of those parental independence experiments. To our surprise, our folks said yes and fronted the hugely expensive four dollars for tickets. They had no earthly clue who or what the band was, a remarkable leap of faith as I consider it now.

On the big night, Mom released us at the front gates of the fair grounds. The camel race arena was a long walk away at the back of the deserted fair grounds. We handed over our tickets and found a place in the rickety wooden stands. The stage, in front of some of the biggest speakers we had ever seen, was plopped in the dirt center of the arena, at best a bleak venue, but everything was new and magical for us. A band came out, but not our band. This was confusing. We had no idea about opening acts. They were loud rockers, long-haired hippies, as Dad would call them. Called Floating Bridge, (yeah, I recall the name of my first opening band) the announcer said they were from Seattle. Nothing could have been any more exotic. Seattle? It rains there.

While they were playing, I became aware that we were the only 'kids' in the crowd. All around us were real hippies, long-haired men (or at least men to us), bearded and beaded, wearing broken down leather boots. And beautiful, impossibly sexy to a pre-pubescent boys, young women with straight long hair in diaphanous peasant dresses wearing sandals, layers of jangly bracelets on their arms. These were people we had only seen on TV or in magazine pictures. One hippie down our row was moving his head up and down to the music. I watched him and started doing the same thing. Looking back at him to see if I was doing it right, he looked straight at me, smiled, and nodded in the affirmative. He handed a hand rolled cigarette to his girlfriend. The breeze smelled sweet, kind of like a dry alfalfa field burning.

"Greg, is that pot? Are they smoking pot?"

I had only seen it in movies and TV. Even in junior high, I knew some kids who had tried it. I liked the way it smelled. It seemed dangerous to be so close to someone who was smoking pot. As I looked around, I realized that other adults were giving Greg and me approving looks, more nods and smiles. It felt like these strangers were watching over us, shepherding us into something. I didn't understand but it felt good. We were special and maybe a little cool, too.

Iron Butterfly hopped up onto the stage. We stood and yelled with everyone else. Greg and I knew all their names and faces from hours staring at the album cover. The music started but something was wrong. The songs sounded familiar but different. It had never occurred to me that the track on the album was only one version of a song. I knew nothing about studio recordings and the live Woodstock Album was not out yet, so I didn't get what live meant. Some of my friends played in a little band, but none of their music was recorded. At first, I didn't like it. I wanted to hear the song as I knew it. But no one else seemed to care. Gradually, it came to me that the same band played the songs different every time. This was a head spinning revelation. When I let go of my need to hear the music as I knew it, all the swirling sound and sensations made sense. I got it. This was live music. This is what a real concert is like. Without completely understanding what had shifted for me, I had been transformed.

The final song of the show was the last track on the album. It mostly consists of screaming guitars and feedback (honestly, I call it that now, but I had no idea how they did it then). Sonically, the mythical Iron Butterfly crashes and burns. As the song came to its crescendo, with the lead guitarist, feet spread wide, writhing as he played, two other hippie guys came out in front of the stage with pans filled with liquid. They pulled out their Zippo lighters and lit the fluid at the feet of the guitar player. The lights came down and the song roared to an end, flames rising from the pans. 1968 baby … special effects. We yelled and clapped but when I looked at my watch I saw that we were late and Mom would be waiting outside the gate. One last look at the hippies and we ran all the way to the front of the fairgrounds. I was sure we had blown it. We would never see live music again. When we got to the car, I didn't understand why we were not in trouble. Maybe it was the looks on our faces. It's entirely likely that Mom saw something I did not yet understand. She only asked, "Did you have fun?" Yeah … yeah … we did. Well that, and my life had completely changed.

I am not sure how many times I have seen bands live since that first show. The number is well into the thousands. Boxes of records and generations of stereo equipment have followed me back and forth and up and down the country. I have seen the big bands. Hunted down my missing great white whales like finally seeing Eric Clapton. But mostly, I don't recall the names of bands I have seen. I can catalogue places, dark smoky clubs, converted churches, brutally hot outdoor venues and oddly shaped strip mall blues joints. Most people who see live music stop when they decide they are now adults. Having kids is the big reason. I didn't make any of those so maybe I didn't grow up.

Now it takes something really special to get me in an arena or large venue. I did the well-drugged stadium shows and have stared down at stages where the distant bands are merely dancing dots in the light. Now I spend my time in small clubs watching unknown bands. As often as not, on a weeknight, I am one of a half-dozen swaying souls in tiny bars where the audience is mostly the other bands and their girlfriends or boyfriends. There is something achingly pure about bands that simply want to play, do what they love. On a good week, I see six bands in two different shows. I am a bit of a live band connoisseur but not a snob. I always applaud the effort but still get chills when a group of musicians is genuinely special. One of those amazing band nights in thirty is more than enough to bring me out again. Something in me, that kid from his first rock show, needs to feel that sensation of being part of an act of creation. Why would anyone stop doing that?

Music has saved my life more than once. Sinking into depression, the antidote was often an album cranked up while I danced, playing air guitar, stomping and posing, just for myself. I don't seek gentility or calm when battling with my dark side. I need music that is aggressive to bring out my psychic warrior. Anything without an edge makes me sadder and angrier. With the right music, I am never alone. When my life was in chaos, broke, unemployed, and couch surfing or on the road, music was my soothing cocoon. The huge catalog of songs in my head are markers for places and people and occasions. Drifting with the music, I can travel to a house or apartment or a club that no longer exists. I can spend some time with people I have lost along the way. Music, like smell or taste, is powerfully evocative and a great organizer of memory. A song can be the lit fuse on completely different explosions of memories.

For so many of us, turning points in life fade away. Lesson incorporated; the essence of the moment is eventually lost to time. Few lights burn brightly forever. I was lucky. What I discovered was portable over time. With each generational evolution in music, I have been able to refresh my own musical narrative. Captured aurally, everything around me gets to have its own sound. Even nostalgia can be as fresh as a new discovery because they are all part of the same continuum of music. If ever you need to find me, look for the old dude in the back of the club, softly now, doing a head bob he learned one warm winter night in a place where camels raced.

MOMENTO

AFTER ALMOST EIGHT YEARS of public service in Portland City Hall, I didn't get the parting cake or cocktails. I didn't get to shake hands and thank people. All I got was a call from the commissioner who then left his chief of staff to deal with the details. I was angry. I was sure that I had earned more than a phone call, but politics is brutally transactional, and the word 'friend' has a transitory meaning.

Even retired for a few months I was still angry at my old friend and boss, Commissioner Nick Fish. During my last year, the chaos in City Hall, the endless protests, had badly triggered my PTSD. As a political centrist, I was never going to be a completely welcome soul in the far-left Portland politics. In my mental health crisis, I made some bad decisions and suffered the consequences.

A few weeks after the call, I snuck into the building late one night and boxed up my office belongings to take home. I took pictures of all the rooms in the office and the empty atrium where the protests happened. I even took a picture of my open file drawers loaded with all the past projects I had done. A friend had given me a small glass baseball from Cooperstown full of whiskey. The sealed bottle had been on my desk for years. I popped it open, put my feet on my old desk once more and took a long drink, a toast to myself at least.

How I start things and end things is very important to me. A few months after I left, I got an text from the commissioner. He wanted to meet for early morning coffee on a Sunday. He said he had something for me. I thought about it for a long time and responded that I couldn't meet. Still trying to recover, I didn't have it in me. A few days later, Nick made a public announcement that he had abdominal cancer that was only treatable by chemotherapy. It was bad. I then realized that he wanted to tell me in person before it became public news. I felt awful when I figured out what was really going on. Life lessons keep coming at you. I immediately arranged to go to City Hall to offer my support for his new battle with cancer. It would take all my courage to once again enter the place that had so badly triggered me. When we met, we talked for almost an hour as if nothing had happened between us. Nick never asked me how I was doing. He said he forgot to bring in what he had for me. It remained his secret.

What is the strangest relationship you have ever had? Was it in your family, so you had no choice? Did you have a lover whose very existence in your life now baffles you? Did you once have a boss who you finally figured out was actually a sociopath? No one gets through life without a strange relationship or ten.

When I jumped careers and got into politics, I sampled candidates for Portland city council. I met Nick at a leadership lunch. He was funny, engaged, and energetic. People I barely knew, but respected, said he was a good guy. When, a couple of weeks later, he asked me to work with him on his campaign I was all in. That simple.

Unannounced, I showed up at his first public forum at the Unitarian Church. I watched, listened, and took notes: little details, like how he sat at the table, where he looked when other candidates spoke, and of course, the content of his answers. He had run a tough losing race a few years before, so he was no rookie, but to my eyes he was clearly rusty. After the event ended, I told him I had notes. His response was, "Great, let me buy you sushi." As he woofed down California rolls, we went over my critique in great detail. So began more than an eight-year collaboration.

I have a healthy ego and am also a ninja level introvert. Nick had a robust ego and was a black belt extrovert. I quickly discovered my favorite place at his political events was leaning against the back wall where I could gauge the room and remain mostly invisible. Nick had both the need and skill to somehow connect with almost anyone in a room. I am a wreck if I anticipate any public speaking. Nick got antsy when he wasn't on the dais. This social interaction yin and yang made us almost a perfect match as elected and staffer. My homeruns were watching words I had written cause a palpable impact on a room when they came out of his mouth.

Nick and I were about the same age. Our life story roots could not be more different. Big city and small town. White collar and blue collar. Jazz and punk rock. Fine dining and take-out. True blue liberal and a mostly moderate. But we had lived the same American history. The two of us were a decade, or decades, older than the rest of his staff. As the staff changed, we were the last ones who had been there for his first winning campaign.

While my name is only on one city ordinance, I can look at Nick's list of his most important accomplishments (he wrote and revised that list constantly) and know that several of them started as a scribble on one of my note pads. That's the job. Mostly invisible. Getting to the finish line on some of those accomplishments was not easy. I'm a contrarian. As political operative I am naturally combative. Nick was a consensus guy. Sometimes I turned the volume to 10 knowing he would turn it down to 7. The entire time I was simply trying to avoid the dull, imperceptible hum of 5.

The differences between us could be explosive. Our idiosyncrasies could annoy the hell out of each other. While always a student of politics, working in the belly of the beast, I came to believe that every person who runs for elected office lands somewhere on a narcissism scale. Even the most introverted ones have a need to be seen and heard. While Nick had a good heart, the world and the lives of everyone who worked for him flowed first through his needs. It was what we signed up for, but in heavy doses it got to me. There were a few times we were more like angry brothers in a fight. We yelled at each other behind his closed door. Sometimes, I was wrong. Sometimes, he was wrong. Most often we were both wrong. But like brothers, once the dust settled, we were fine.

One time, after a loud, vigorous discussion that could be heard through his office door, if not walls, I walked out of his office door feeling fine. I looked around the office to see a collection of horrified faces. Not one of the other team members could even imaging yelling at 'The

Commissioner.' I smiled and reassured them. "Good meeting."

The last Christmas I worked with Nick, he invited what we called TeamFish up to his family apartment for a 'holiday' party. What no one but my wife knew was that I almost drove away. My nervous system was on high alert by that time. If a parking place hadn't opened in front of us, I was gone. I willed myself into the elevator and made a beeline to the wine glasses when we arrived. At one point, I went down the hall to the bathroom. Just inside one of the rooms was a small table with a baseball mounted on a stand in a protective cover. I didn't touch it but leaned down to see who had signed it. Sometime later in the evening, I said to Nick in passing something like, "Very cool baseball."

With Nick, you were sometimes unsure if you left a lasting impact on him. He was restless and tended to focus on who and what was right in front of him. A few weeks after our City Hall meeting, I went to see one of his reelection forums. I took my customary station at the back of the room. His face was narrowed and drawn in a shocking way. I had seen him do those sorts of public events hundreds of times. If strangers couldn't tell, I knew he was exhausted but in front of the meager audience he was still on his game. That moment in front of a few people sitting on folding chairs, almost always an act of joy in his job before, was clearly an enormous act of will. I found myself both wanting the event to end and rooting for him every time he spoke. I was seeing the last hurrah of a good man, and as my own ghosts were shunted aside, I was wishing for things I knew could not be. Afterwards, he worked the room and then made his way over to me. While shaking his hand, I was thinking, *Geez, Nick you need to get home and rest now*. He made a big deal about having some things for me.

More than a big deal, there was an urgency in his voice. I set up a time with his scheduler and went down to City Hall a couple of days later.

One of the first things I did for Nick was staff the discussions that pushed my beloved Portland Beavers, and baseball, out of town and brought in the Timbers soccer team, a sport I detest. I was mortified and angered. I have never recovered. When I used to go to games at Civic Stadium and see old guys keeping score, I would tell friends, "Look at those guys. That is my retirement." Endless 'celebrations' of soccer in City Hall were fingernails on my baseball blackboard. I have not set foot in the stadium since the Beavers left. What would be the point? A handful of the dirt from around home plate of the last game is in a plastic bag on my desk. A relic in my personal baseball shrine.

Door to his office closed, I sat across from Nick on his too low Ikea couch and he brought out a plastic shopping bag. First, he handed me a signed first edition of a baseball book called *Slide!* (Nick collected first editions … so this was a big deal.) He then told me he knew I would never recover from losing the Beavers, but he had found some things in his endless bookstore rambles that might help. First, he gave me a written and pictorial history of the Beavers (very cool) and, I have no idea where he found this, an official 2002 Portland Beavers program. Funny thing is, I was so poor when I started to go to Beavers games that I didn't buy the program. I could only afford the lineup/scorecard for 50 cents. The program had me on the edge of tears.

As we talked about the books, he kept one hand in the bag. Then he said, "I have a family of soccer fans and I wanted this to be with someone who would appreciate it and take good care of it." Out came the baseball I had seen in his apartment. The ball was signed to his father, the congressman, "For Cong. Fish—With Best Wishes—Fay Vincent." Vincent was the commissioner of baseball. What I hadn't seen the first time was that the ball was stamped OFFICIAL BALL 1991 ALL-STAR GAME. And real baseball fans will get the importance of this; the ball was rubbed in and appeared to be game used.

My relationship with Nick was one of the strangest of my life. But don't confuse strange with bad. From his journey to Portland politics to my dumping a long, completely different, career to chase a political dream, almost everything about our time together was improbable. Still, somehow, we managed to leave indelible marks on each other's lives. Such is the immutable truth of people who enable each other's dreams. As I parted, I did something that had never happened between us before. I slipped by his offered hand and gave the Commissioner a hug.

During all our time together, I wrote the drafts for his major speeches. Both good, but very different writers, we argued points draft after draft. He always won. After all, it was his speech. I wrote the first version of this essay not long after he gave me the ball and published it for him to read. After reading it, he texted back a single line, one that he knew would be the greatest honor he could bestow in our relationship. "You were always the better writer."

I got to celebrate my writing collaboration with Nick Fish one last time. He fought the disease for over two years, working at the job he loved until a month before he passed away. At the enormous memorial service, one of the speakers began to describe a speech that I wrote with Nick.

Every year, only he and I worked on his biggest speech of the year. He delivered the closing remarks to a room of about 1,000 educators, high school parents, and their families at a constitutional competition where he was always a judge. I started drafting that yearly speech months in advance so we could revise and revise it again. He always asked me to come up with the subject. One year, after Oregon had legalized recreational marijuana, I wrote a draft about pot and how our new law was a state's rights issue. He tilted his head and gave me a worried look when he started reading the first draft but came around when he saw how I made it all about the constitution.

One speaker at the memorial was the educator who ran that yearly competition. She told a story about Nick giving those speeches and said, "I especially recall the time he began a speech by saying he was going to talk about legalizing marijuana. I looked at all those kids and their parents and was horrified." The room erupted in laughter. Unable to contain my tears, I looked at my wife and said, "I think my speech just got a laugh at Nick's memorial." He would have liked that.

RINGING

Silence. I have no idea what that is like. I think silence might be wonderful but as a child I eliminated that possibility. Mind you, not on purpose, but relentlessly, nonetheless. Especially in my left ear, I suffer from raging tinnitus, ringing in the ears. They say ringing, but that isn't quite it. It isn't a hiss, but it isn't the endless note of bell either. The sound isn't a note I can recall hearing in music, but I bet a musician could replicate it. The sound is sharp, a tornado through a keyhole. If I pay attention to it, the noise will blot out even the loudest outside sounds. My right ear has a slightly lower tone that I have to concentrate to hear because the left is so loud. Constantly surrounding myself with sound—be that music or the rushing air of a fan—is a feeble attempt to reclaim my aural world.

There was a time when we all assumed that loud noise was merely a transient exterior problem. Once the sound stopped, we would be fine. That sounds so crazy now, but there you go. You don't know what you don't know.

I attribute my relentless internal noise to three things. An early gift from my dad was a single shot .22 rifle. Laborious to load, it was considered the perfect kid's gun, a safe way to learn how to handle a firearm. Even one by one, I could easily burn through 100 rounds plinking at cans and posts. Good clean fun. We thought our ears were bullet proof. No one remotely considered hearing protection. If you are a right hander, your left ear is lined up to take the sound shot. Right cheek against the rifle, sighting down the barrel, your left ear is hanging in the air, a perfect sound receptor. Bang … bang … bang and the dull ringing in my ear would start. No matter, it eventually went away.

Lacking air conditioning in my car, I drove with the driver's window open. Thousands and thousands of miles, from one side of the country to the other, from top to bottom of America, wind and the sound of other cars beat away at my left ear.

"I can't hear!" From my teens, concert after concert, this was our shared cry as we walked out of the arena. We were proud of our transitory hearing loss because it was a shared experience. Not hearing meant we had heard the bands. Hundreds of shows … hundreds. One night may have been the final sonic hammer to my left ear. Blame it on Jack Daniels and a local band called the Razorbacks in a tiny bar. A buddy was leaving town. He bought several rows of shots of Jack and had the waitress put them on the table in neat lines. Generally, in any live venue, I scope out the sound board and park myself in front of it, away from the monitors, so the music is balanced. My friend had picked a little table next to the stage-right speakers. Sitting across from him, my left ear was but feet from the blast. I knew it was stupid. I knew it was too loud. I knew I was fucking up. But as I did all those shots and I didn't want to dampen the joy of my buddy's last night I stayed in that seat. Sitting down in my car later, my left ear was in pain. After that, I never went to a show without earplugs … in time to save what was left of my hearing.

Ever have a problem that doesn't seem like a problem until it creates another problem? Okay, that was hard to follow. I once blew a disk in my back so badly that I had to have surgery. The pain, as it often is in such cases, was in the shin of my left leg. For six months, I felt the equivalent of someone taking a hacksaw to my left shin. Finally, I had surgery and got lucky. It was a perfect fix. My back was fine, except I had to teach myself how to walk again. In response to the shin pain, my foot discovered that it hurt a little less if it pointed at a 45-degree outward angle. Duck-like. I never noticed what my foot had decided until I began to walk after the surgery. I felt unbalanced and looked down to see my left foot wanting to go a different direction. It took a month of conscious walking for it to join the rest of my body and go the same direction with us.

My tinnitus wasn't a problem until I began to explore silence. For my sanity, I learned meditation. The sitting I got. The controlled breathing … check. Letting the physical discomfort come and go … okay. The reward … silence … *what?* I had no silence. The quieter my meditation location, the louder my tinnitus. In book after book, writers told me about the wonderful reward of silence, the place where one could observe thoughts and experience little slices of timelessness. I had no idea what they were talking about. "Follow your breath." Sure, right after I find a place to hide from the damn screaming in my head. Surely, I thought, there must be a way to deal with this. I need to be silent.

In the midst of a sinus infection, I went to a specialist.

Maybe the noise was related to my aching sinuses. Fix one, fix the other? Life is a steady diet of false hope. After sending a small snake into my nostrils and writing a prescription, the doctor said, "You know. We could test your hearing today, too." Sure. He had a soundproof booth and a tech to twiddle knobs on the other side of the glass. Later, I wondered how often a day he said, "Test your hearing." Lots of billable hours in that little room. Still, though he had warned me there wasn't really any science to repair those damaged little hairs in my ear it seemed reasonable to know, as he said, "how bad it is."

I put on headphones. The tech started creating different tones. He told me the trick was to find a tone that matched the one in my head. Right side first. I pointed my thumb up or down to find the frequency. When I gave the okay, the tech turned up the volume and like magic the sound in my head disappeared. Volume up and down. Up and down, until I saw him right down a number. Through the glass, I saw the doctor come in the room. He smiled and gave me thumbs up. I was not sure why. Left ear. Same test. The matching tone had a higher pitch. Okay, got it. Then, incrementally, the blocking volume went up. Thumbs down. Up again. Down again. I saw the Dr. and tech exchange a glance.

Now, sound once again in both ears, a voice, "You still hear the tinnitus now?"

"Yup," I said.

Little head shakes in the booth. One more adjustment and finally my noise disappeared in both ears. The tech came in took the headphones.

"Mr. Blackwood, that was remarkable. Your hearing is pretty good but the tinnitus in your left ear is off the charts.

Sorry, but there isn't really anything we can do about that."

Earplugs in, the band blasts the first notes. Bass and ripping drums pushing the air in my lungs. The music is safely outside my ears. I hear everything I need well enough to be happy. While there are a few people in the room with earplugs, I look around and see all the exposed ears and I wonder what they are hearing. Carefully, I pull the right earplug, never left, a little bit out of my ear. Holy shit! That is fucking loud. Then, for fun, I concentrate on my own sound in my left ear. Ah, there it is. Is it? Yup, it is louder than the music in the room. Then I let go of my sound and go back to the music.

This is the trick I learned after years of meditation. I can choose 'not hearing.' First, I had to let go of my frustration that I would never experience silence. That was a drag. I imagine silence as a special place slightly beyond the horizon of my consciousness. It must be nice there. I wish I remembered it and could hear my breath all the way deep into my lungs and out again. It must be easier to concentrate, to let the mind wander. Those Zen monks like to talk about the power of the silence. That used to annoy me, but I let go of the jealousy. So, I kept sitting and breathing and trying not to take a ride on my thoughts. Slowly, I discovered I could feel my breath, the coolness as it flowed over the moist membranes in my nose. I noticed the way my belly fell as my diaphragm rose. The slight movement of ribs as my lungs expanded, and the nuanced release of my muscles as the warm breath crossed back out of my nose. I didn't have to hear my breath. I could feel it, the physical act of breathing over and over as the noise in my ears kept to itself.

Something mysterious happened. I began to hear my

breath, the flow of the air in and out was louder than the sound in my ears. I no longer had to segregate the annoying sound from my meditation. I could breathe through it and around it. The sound that never goes away disappeared.

I still don't know what silence is, but I do know how to create it.

PORNO

I SPENT ABOUT AN HOUR hanging around outside a porno theater. I have this thing about photographing buildings right before they disappear. The sign out front, one of those cheap, backlit yellowing plastic types, used to say, 'Oregon Theater: Films For Mature Adults.' But the neighborhood fixture since the 1970s has been sold and the new owner covered the original sign with a banner that only says, 'Oregon Theater.' I stared at the new sign for a long time wondering if the owners were somehow embarrassed that they bought the place. Still, proudly hanging in one of the double glass front doors was a poster with a picture of the front of the place featuring the original sign. Someone is conflicted.

The theater has been an absent-minded fixture in my life for over three decades. A place you see so often that you stop seeing it. Taking up half of a short block, the theater is down the street from my favorite family run hardware store. Closer still to the bar where on hot summer days I indulged in the best gin and tonic I have ever had. The bartenders made their own tonic. I have no idea how one would begin to do such a thing, but I was grateful every sip. The flavor alone compelled me to drink beyond my lightweight tolerance. The bar closed so the world has been deprived of the best ever gin and tonic. I still long for the nobly named Victory Gin.

When I arrived in Portland in the mid 1980s, it was generally acknowledged as the pornography capital of America. Oregon has an expansive free speech provision in the state constitution. Fully naked dancing for tips is considered free speech. Who knew? Adult entertainment shops and theaters dotted most of the major thoroughfares in the inner-city neighborhoods. I walked by one of the most infamous peek-show houses every day on the way to work. On my way home, a sort of barker/security guy stood just outside the door. He walked the exceedingly fine line between beckoning and threatening.

I have never been inside a porno theater. I am not sure why. I was curious about what they were like inside and I often follow my curiosity where it leads me. I was press-ganged to a strip club for my bachelor's party and once went into an upscale shop full of fancy sex toys and devices. Interesting, but they didn't have anything I needed at the time. I think the one thing that kept me out of those theaters was the look of the guys I saw entering them. I can't say I have ever seen anyone enter one of those establishments with anything I would call confidence. The men I saw adopted a posture that I can only call furtive, sort of the aspect a grazing deer, nervous and ready to run at the slightest noise. Then there was 'the look,' the quick scan by those men of everything and everyone around them as they reached for the door handle. I guess it wasn't a see and be seen thing. I never wanted to be that guy.

As I do often do when I photograph a dying building, I did some research. Seems the place has been called the Oregon Theater since it opened in 1925. I liked that. I like continuity, it's reassuring. It had a Wurlitzer pipe organ and a vaudeville stage with about 700 seats. I have been in much smaller neighborhood theaters of the same vintage. By all accounts, this one was never grand. The long oatmeal colored brick fronting the avenue is little adorned. In fact, without a sign one would never know it was a theater at all. It wasn't a movie palace. There's a certain progression for theaters like this one. Live acts and vaudeville, much loved local movie house, decaying home of fine arts and foreign films, then destitute porno house. To the building's credit, it made it through all of the phases without being torn down.

While looking for photograph angles to take advantage of the sharp low winter sun, I watched three serious looking young men, tape measures on their belts, clipboards in their hands, go in and out of the theater, then move down the block to a second entrance I had never noticed. Hanging out into a street above that door obscured by tree branches was another faded plastic sign. Next to a shriveled 7-Up soda logo, it read: ID TAVERN – BINGO SAT. 5:00 – Free Pool 5-7 MON. TUES. WED. FRI. Frozen in time like that, the sign was both sad and optimistic. Standing under it, clicking away with my camera, I wondered, *Sunday we rest, but what happened on THURS?*

ID. The id? Freud? That's the random junk that fills my brain. The sign has to be a couple of decades old, maybe older. This was a mostly blue-collar street in the heyday of the ID TAVERN. There were no cookie cutter modern apartment blocks hulking over the narrow, two-lane avenue back then. Could the name really be that literal? You had to have an ID to get in the joint. The sign isn't long for this world and I am pretty sure I am the only one pondering this mystery.

There is another sort of happy ending that can happen in these houses of many happy endings. The Oregon has a sister called The Aladdin. It fell on hard times and at the end of its decay cycle gained some notoriety for setting the record for the longest continuous run of one movie: *Deep Throat*. More than a decade did that classic movie keep bringing in patrons. Since then the Aladdin remade itself into a first-class music and comedy venue. Even that hard won transition bothers me.

I have often found myself sitting in the Aladdin waiting for the opening act, musing as I looked around the small theater at the rows of old-fashioned wooden back seats and then down at the clean grey-painted floor. *Good lord, what must have been on these floors when they began cleaning this place up the first time?* I muse. Anyone who has had the joy of great sex knows that it is delightfully messy. Fluids fly everywhere with gleeful abandon. Mattresses, over time, can become a landscape of past adventures. (Think twice about that used mattress, kids.) So, if over a decade of men went to see, and let's assume no one ever saw *Deep Throat* in its entirely, there doesn't seem to be any way that the floor had not became the resting place for generations of, shall we say, deposits. Were there rules, a shared code? Were there tissue boxes liberally scattered around the room? Or was it like a pick-up baseball game where you are expected to bring your own mitt? In the end, the urge had to overcome the etiquette, don't you think? Yeah, I can't sit quietly and chat with friends. I always end up staring at the floor of the theater and speculating. It's a problem.

As buildings are abandoned or are merely empty waiting for the next long-term lease, a plague of urban locusts descends. Text messages fire up, and in the night, mostly young men, dressed in black hoodies to avoid cameras, backpacks loaded with markers and cans of spray paint, descend on the innocent building. Graffiti has become an urban plague. It only takes days for empty buildings to be completely covered in tags small and enormous, detailed and scrawled. The text itself is a language known only to a few. They are talking to each other, not to the rest of us. Beyond the blight, there is a certain narcissism to the tagging. I have read that when caught, taggers claim they can't help themselves. They become addicted to the thrill of the hunt, the possibility of being caught in the act, and the self-satisfaction that in the daylight they alone know what they have done.

Some new owners of abandoned buildings have tried to prevent the graffiti onslaught by offering their walls to artists who paint murals, good and bad, interesting and mundane. For a time, the taggers seemed to respect the wall art. There is some truth that many wall muralists were once, or continue to be, taggers who have discovered a community honoring outlet for their impulses. But compulsion is hard. Lately, a new switch has been thrown, a lawlessness among the lawless. Tags are appearing on top of murals. A downward spiral of mixed messages.

The outside walls of the Oregon Theater became a home for new wall art now being slowly degraded. I wonder, though, if I have found birds of a feather. I think of those many men who with a quick survey of the street, slipped into the doors of the theater for a brief afternoon or evening expression of delight. In many ways, they really aren't that much different from the night stalking taggers out looking for a quick hit of adrenaline in a sprayed paint swirl. Neither is so ashamed that they will stop. They crave the act. No, they both become secret agents of pleasure embracing stealth to reach their personal places of happiness and relief. Impulses sated; they can later stroll the boulevard perhaps smirking as they gaze upon the shared landmark of their efforts. My bet is that they both are going to miss the shady incarnation of the Oregon Theater: Films for Mature Adults.

EXPOSED

———————————

IN WASHINGTON DC, just behind the Library of Congress, is the Folger Shakespeare Library. Near the entrance is a statue of Puck the narrator of *A Midsummer Night's Dream*. Puck's arm points lazily toward the Capitol Building in the distance and inscribed below him is the line, "Lord, what fools these mortals be!" The first time I saw it, I laughed out loud. Perfect. That little statue and Shakespeare's line came back to me as, for the first time, I held the proof copy of my memoir. At slightly over a pound, suddenly my words had substance, actual heft. I teared up a bit as I weighed the book in my hand and thought, *Oh shit. What have I done?*

Writing a memoir is like being sealed into a huge snow globe with one's life and choosing to have a giant, standing mute, shake it over and over. At times disconcerting and emotionally taxing, I soon got used to the isolation both inside my mind and in the room where I clicked away at the keyboard. The stories popped into my head and I cheerfully wrote them. Alone in my thoughts, I hadn't fully registered that my effort would have an audience. One day, my editor sent me a question asking me to think about how the reader would understand a paragraph. *The reader?* My comfortable snow globe slipped from the giant's hand and shattered on to the floor. Bits and pieces went everywhere. Little plastic flakes of stories splashed and drizzled in every direction.

Writing is an almost monastic endeavor. I had a couple of early readers of the first draft. As friends, fully acquainted with my flaws and idiosyncrasies, they were helpful and kind to both the text and me. They were also safe. Even my wife had not read the read the entire manuscript until I shipped it off to my editor, a professional stranger.

To be sure, chapter by chapter, I thought about the people I thought might want to read about how their stories intersected with mine. They became mini muses as I scrolled through the timeline of my life. For the good times, I enjoyed spending time with those friends again. Our lives and passions became real, propelling me forward. In the tough times, catharsis was the coaxing muse.

A memoir can be a powerful device to correct the record. I began the work with a vow to squeeze as much truth as I could from my memory and give it to the pages. It isn't much of an effort to write a better story of one's life. This is something we all do, this replaying of events with different words, places, and outcomes. I took moments from my life and ran them backward and forward like a YouTube video. Things I didn't understand at the time were suddenly clear. Everyone makes good and bad choices, leaves joyful and awful impressions in our wake. We hurt people while not intending to and embrace people we should have avoided. Alas, there is no rewind or pause button in life.

One thing relentlessly leads to another. Bricks are layered into our tower of experience, no matter how solid the underlying structure. I would fantasize about how my own revelations would offer redemption if only people from my past read my book. "Ah," I would think, "if they could read this and understand what was really going on way back then I could have resolution."

But that is 'inside the snow globe' thinking, isn't it? Not everything in our lives is important to everyone else. Each person is creating his or her own leaning tower of experience. The bricks we may think are essential, foundational, may only be carelessly laid remnants for someone else. Even knowing this is true didn't decrease my hope that certain people would find the book and, good lord the hubris, be enlightened about me.

Before anyone else knew it was available, I loaded my new tome on Amazon. I typed in the title and my nascent book appeared on my screen. It's a heady experience the first time you see culmination of over a year's effort alive in the digital landscape. As I was tapping through pages on my eReader, looking for any formatting issues, I realized the book was shockingly new to me. Everyone's eyes and brain have a certain detachment as a reader. If you are lucky, you may be transformed by the words of a stranger. As I read my book, I suddenly had the reader's expectation. I thought, *Well, that was well written. Good sentence. Nice transition. That could have been written better. That's sad. That's funny. What's coming next?* These seem like absurd thoughts for the author, someone who wrote those sentences and read them ten … fifteen … 100 times. I was confused. The medium became the message. My well-honed reader's distance reminded me what a crazy thing I had done.

The exposure started simply. A guy I had grown up with but lost track of decades ago contacted me on social media. A message popped up. I could tell he was trying to tell me something about my book, but reading and rereading what he said I had no idea what he was trying to convey. An eccentric fellow when I knew him, at first, I thought he was going for a bizarre, failed attempt at wit. I was baffled until a second message came from him referring to a chapter in my book. I looked again at his first message. Holy shit! That's me. He was quoting me back to me. Out of context, I didn't recognize the words that I had written, a paragraph he had found personally meaningful.

While in flights of fancy I imagined my book would reach thousands, I knew it would be read a small cadre of friends and family, and with luck, a few strangers. An introvert who spent a lifetime seeking a small group of close friends, I succeeded too well. From that closely held seedbed, a second layer of people appeared, one-time friends and former coworkers. But even from that small collection the impact was immediate and overwhelming. My memoir, raw in places, became a permission slip for others to reveal intimate details about their lives. Strangers offered me intensely personal stories. I suppose my openness made me seem safe or at least someone who would understand. I had not expected this new accumulation of unfiltered intimacy. It gradually made me feel anxious and overwhelmed. While I have spent a lifetime talking to therapists, I had never experienced what that must be like for them. My therapist told me that I had opened the door and now my new job, the safe one, was active acknowledgement, not problem solving.

There is a precariousness in choosing to expose oneself. Truth is, very few people wake up one day and say, "I need to write a book and tell my life." That may mean I am now among the unbalanced few. The reward for such audacity could be a billowing ego. But then there is the anchor, the moment that slays all hubris. Even the most successful writer returns to the empty page, the blank screen, the void that mocks self-importance.

A dear friend marveled at the emotional risk I had taken to write about my screwed up and wonderful life. I thanked him, genuinely humbled. But later, back at my keyboard, I realized that the only moment it ever felt risky to reveal myself was when I first felt the weight of the book in my hand. That feeling passed quickly as I fanned pages under my thumb. Turns out, in the end I didn't feel so much exposed as free. It was as if all those little plastic snowflakes in the broken globe didn't lay on the ground in a puddle. No, as the sun dried them and a breeze stirred, they took flight.

OUTSIDE

—————————

WHEN I WORKED FOR A CITY COMMISSIONER, I was his liaison to the Parks and Recreation department. There are over 150 parks in Portland, including the largest urban natural area in America—Forest Park. The natural area encompasses over 3,000 acres and is considered the jewel of the parks system. I know this because I wrote the commissioner's speeches and never failed to call the park 'the jewel.' I spent hundreds of hours in meetings talking about Forest Park, planning the park, enhancing the park, and protecting it. I spent days in a room with the members of an achingly passionate non-profit named after the park. I validated and supported the opinions and pleas of all the members with nods and smiles. I fought for more funding for the park and ways to make it even more accessible to everyone in the city. I gladly received the praise for the seriousness of my advocacy for nature in the city. I was one of them. Except … in my over three decades in Portland I have never been to Forest Park. Hell, I wouldn't be caught dead on those endless winding trails.

People love to tell me about hiking. Hiking. Walking out in some direction and back. I watch the news. Sometimes hikers don't come back. People go for a 'day hike' and then disappear, only to be found days later licking water off leaves to stay alive. "They weren't properly equipped," some uber outdoorsy looking dude solemnly says into the camera when they find the missing soul alive … or dead.

Outdoor equipment? Now you're talkin'. I love to go to those big stores full of roughing it gear. Oh, the wonderful gadgets. The tiny stoves and cozy little tents, the dried food in bags you boil and the wonderful boots and socks. Good lord, Gore-Tex, dry and breathable. What's not to love? I actually have good boots and Gore-Tex jackets. I use them to walk in the rain between where I park my car and any building I enter. You don't have to hike to buy real cool stuff.

My wife is a great earthquake prepper. We are ready for the big one. We have MREs and gluten free one-bag meals we ordered from Utah … always Utah. We have nice sleeping bags, compact plates and cutlery, assorted lamps, a wind-up radio, waterproof matches, a tent, plastic ponchos, water purifying tablets, a toilet in a five-gallon bucket, and a little stove. The doomsday cache is in a couple of galvanized trash cans at the top of our driveway, just beyond the collapse range of our house which, at my wife's urging, we have bolted to the foundation, but based on where we put the cans, we still think the house will fall over anyhow. None of the stash has ever been out of its original packaging. In a real disaster, we would have to read the instructions for the stove and tent. I have rolled out a few sleeping bags in my day. I am a veteran. And I'm pretty sure that the food in those sealed bags is perfect for a disaster, a time when you don't have any choice but to eat what you have. I haven't actually tasted any of the food. I want to be desperately hungry to first try them. I think if I knew what they tasted like I would be less sure about survival.

If you grow up in a small town in the middle of nowhere nature is unavoidable. I enjoyed our family day trips up into the mountains where all us kids climbed rocks and beheld the miracle of naturally flowing water. While my family camped, I don't recall anyone waxing lyrical about being in nature. (When did we start saying 'in nature?') I am not sure we camped for the wilderness at all. We liked the trees and smell of pine sap and the joy of starting a fire and burning stuff. We had a big tent and later a camper for Dad's pickup. That's the thing, for us, camping was always something that happened after you got out of a car or a truck or climbed off a motorcycle. The kinds of places we camped first required some skill with backing a vehicle into a narrow campsite, surrounded by other skillfully backed vehicles. We packed pretty much like we were preparing for the apocalypse. Everything came but the television.

For my family, camping wasn't so much about nature as it was a tightly mitigated inconvenience. We were thrust upon each other in small spaces, a tent or a camper. We jostled and skootched around each other to eat and sleep. Sleeping especially was all about process and space allocation, the patterns of sleeping bags to fill a tent, or the careful disassembly of the little dining table in the camper to magically turn it into a too-short bed where my younger brother and I elbowed and kicked each other all night.

Then there were the restrooms. Once the vehicles were nicely aligned in the allotted spaces and the always a bit miniaturized gear distributed to its new home, I set out to find the restroom. Whether the large communal restrooms of the bigger campsites or the more primitive outhouses, you could pretty much follow your nose to the facilities. Even as a scrawny kid I knew enough to be sad for the families, late to the show, whose campsites were closest to the restrooms. There was no way for them not to whiff the unmistakable stench of human shit and piss nor ignore the endless stream of souls hurrying in and strolling out. At night, for the restroom last call, we got to carry flashlights. In normal life there is rarely call for a flashlight. Oh, everyone has them, hanging in the basement, garage, or rolling around a kitchen drawer, but think about it, how many times do you actually use a flashlight? Mostly, they sit unloved, batteries slowly draining away to disappoint you in the moment you actually need a light.

For a kid, a flashlight in the dark of a campsite is pure joy. The beam showed us where to walk. Aimed into the unlit night sky, I used to imagine that my little light would somehow stay a tight beam and head off into the heavens unrestrained by atmosphere. I was sure that someone in space could see the blink of my flashlight as I turned it on and off in long and short pulses like Morse Code. My flashlight beam would send its message unstoppable into the heavens. But then I would hear a rustle in the trees and quickly my light performed its most important task, keeping me safe from all sorts unknown things that go bump in the night.

Camping was fun, an adventure. It was always something I wanted to do and I was always sad when it was time to pack and go back home. It was better than being stuck in the back seat on the long trip from Southern California to see my dad's family in Arkansas. Once, our folks tricked my brother and me by saying that on the way home from our last trip to the Ozarks we would camp in exotic places like New Mexico and Colorado. We carefully packed all the camping gear in a huge metal footlocker and tied it to the top of the massive Pontiac station wagon. There, above our heads, mile after mile, was hope of a bright future, a reason to endure the boredom of endless miles. But we never opened the box. The closest we got to it was tying and retying the ropes that held it down. In Arkansas, Mom got sick. Explained to us as 'women's problems,' it was clear to me she was somehow enduring excruciating pain all the way home. We didn't camp, but we did see deep canyons, high bridges, and the continental divide. Mom was game, but my heart wasn't in it. It wasn't anything like camping and I was empathic enough to see her suffering. At some point, the meandering ended, and we made a high-speed run for home. The heavy camping box came down off the car unopened.

When I was old enough to have my own car, I thought about camping. I went to the sporting goods store and got my own camping stuff. My goal was to have everything I needed to spontaneously go camping and fit it into one half of the trunk of my underpowered, thin metal box Toyota Corolla. Everything had to fit in a cooler with enough room for a small tent beside it. All I had to do was grab my sleeping bag, food, water, and be gone. I liked the idea that I was so self-contained. I used to open my trunk and show people my camping gear in that tiny space. They were inevitably impressed. Thinking about it now, I am not sure why I created that kit. Maybe l mostly liked the plan. Some sort of survivalist. Truth was, I almost never used my gear.

I know I never went camping by myself. Those were the early days of my emerging Panic Disorder. The pervasive disease had not manifested yet, but I was already developing an overriding need for caution, being ready. For what? I never knew. My car, the independence it gave me, was my ultimate safe place and the means to escape. I liked being an entity to myself, or more correctly, I liked the illusion I created.

At college, there were a few times I actually used my kit on weekend runs with my new girlfriend. Turns out my camping gear plan worked. I think the last time I actually camped was a trip with her down the west coast from the mouth of the Columbia River to LA. That experience was wonderful: fog in the Redwoods, deer in our camp on a finger of land pointing toward the ocean, and rolling breakers lighting up with phosphorescence. So wonderful that I never camped again.

The reason I could fool all those Forest Park nature types was that I actually know the calming solace of nature. Even now, I can spend uncounted time sitting on my haunches watching an ant hill. Moving water is spellbinding. The interminable motion and white noise detach my nervous mind from my innards. I am perfectly happy reflecting on how the branches of a Giant Sequoia reach like tentacles into the sky. I check the newly tilled soil in my garden several times a day waiting for the first green probe to crack the surface in my dahlia bed. I have a special tree, an early bloomer, that I watch day by day to see when the buds begin to get chubby telling me spring is on the way. But outside … beyond an umbilical to civilization … nope.

My wife used to go camping for a week with her sister's

family. I would stay home with the dogs. One time, they chose a new location, close to a small town. I always knew I was missing something and started to look for a way to be part of that experience. But not in the way you are thinking. No, I looked for hotel, close to the campsite where I could stay each night. I wanted to be a nature tourist who kept one foot in a city. I imagined I would wake up at a reasonable hour, grab breakfast in a greasy spoon, and then head over to hang with the campers during the day, even into the evening and dinner. Then I would doff my cap, kiss my wife goodbye, head back to the hotel, and put my feet up on the couch to watch the local news. Do I have to say that never happened? Of course not. That's insane.

I never figured out how to be outside … all the way outside. My nervous system creates a bubble, a cocoon really, only visible to me. It tells me that beyond the edge of my little world is danger. Like the first maps of the oceans, with the unknown edges and beyond marked, "thar be dragons." I can drive to a trailhead, head off into the distance but always … always … at some unseen point, my mind starts doing a calculation that goes something like this: *Hold it, have I gone too far? Have I reached the point of no return? How long will it take me to walk back from here? Can I walk that far? What if something happens? Can I get to safety?* No return? Pretty dramatic, eh?

That inner dialogue starts as a whisper but each step away from my car the inner voice gets louder and louder. My busy eyes stop looking outward and I begin doing the return journey calculations. The hike becomes a death march. At that point I am no longer outside, not really. I am in the most inside place anyone can ever be, stuck in my own head. Every natural impulse is to turn around and get my ass back into my safety bubble where I belong.

But humans compensate, adjust, and create new realities. When I bought my first home, I became what I never imagined I would be: a gardener. Growing up, working in the yard was more like a punishment, but when the grass and the plants were mine, I developed a relationship with them. I trimmed and tilled and fertilized. Every day, in all the seasons, I look around to see what each shrub, tree, or flower is doing. I sit for hours staring at my yard and garden, imaging what I will do next, what color, what texture. Or I imagine wholesale changes, paths and rocks and entirely new tiers for flowers and vines and ground cover. In many ways, this close-up relationship with nature is far more intimate than the flood of sights of a hike in the woods or desert.

I am often mistaken for a solely urban creature because I don't hike or camp or snowshoe or kayak. I get it. I live in a city where everyone seems to have an outside life, one with tales to tell. I understand the confusion. They live for the big outside, a place I only like to visit in small, sequestered doses. In many ways, I spend more hours in my little outside. It is just beyond my back door and there will be no search parties if I disappear.

THEATERS

Do you have a holy place? A redoubt where you feel most like yourself, uplifted, relaxed, engaged? Is it a place where you sometimes get that little shudder that starts at the top of your head and wiggles down your body all the way to your toes? When you are in your special place do you know that in a flash any emotion can break loose and sink you down in your seat fighting back tears or have you leaning forward with a smile so wide that your lips hurt?

I have never had this experience in a church. As a child, stuck in the pews of a Baptist Church, I counted the minutes until I could leave. I read the Sunday Program over and over. I liked the announcements of tragedy. Sick and dying church members in need of prayer seemed real, or at least interesting. Even then, sensitive to the timber of music, the out-of-tune droning of hymns was painful. And the soloists, moved by the Lord, were mostly awful. I wondered if they knew how bad they were and why they would hold themselves up for ridicule. No applause in the conservative church, they walked down from behind the pulpit to smiles and nods, which seemed about right, but when that rare singer showed actual talent, the reaction from the pews was the same, a sitting ovation.

I never saw my parents as religious. Nothing in my life seemed particularly spiritual. One Sunday, people who were 'moved by the Lord' got in a line along the wall to go up to the pulpit and tell everyone about their blessings. I was shocked when my dad got up and joined the line. I kept looking at him in line wondering what he would say. When his turn came, he talked about how he was blessed to have a successful business to take care of his family. Of course, not so much moved as transactional. Don't tempt fate. I don't think it was so much about being blessed as grateful, and there was nothing wrong with that. His parents where scions of the church, genuinely holy people. I think he felt a little pressure to meet expectations. Actually, I think that is the reason my brother and I were at church at all. Generation after generation we never stop trying to please our parents. At last, the service would end, and I could escape. But not without shaking the hand of the preacher. His hand was pink, squishy, and a little damp. I hated it— his hand—not him.

There were three places in my little town where people gathered under high ceilings: the church, the school gyms, and the Aladdin Theater. Indifferent to religion and hopeless in any sort of athletics, the movie theater was where I first found my heart. The Aladdin was our version of an old-style movie house. The Aladdin's Lamp theme went with the dunes that surrounded us in every direction. Truth is, buildings, streets, and schools all latched onto what I suppose were then called 'Oriental' references. My high school mascot was a Rajah; our nearby rival, the Arabs.

Street names came from varieties of date palms. So, having a theater on the short main drag in Indio decorated with the tale of Aladdin made sense, kind of. When I got to college one of my best friends came from Blythe, another anonymous desert town ninety miles from Indio on the Colorado River. I was gob smacked when he told me that when he and his friends wanted to go to a movie, they drove the from Blythe to Indio and back. It was unimaginable to think that Indio was, for him, the center of film culture.

Once in the double front doors of the Aladdin, the snack bar was immediately in front of us. On both sides of the foyer were entrances that looped to the middle of the theater like arms reaching out to hug the big room. As a child, those halls were mysterious. A place for adults. Shiny, painted concrete, cool, smooth to the touch, decorated with palm trees and strange made-up Arab symbols. On one side of each walkway was a sort of shelf. Every few feet were small square wells filled with sand. While in those days people could smoke in the theater, to my child's eyes the ritual was for adults to smoke one last cigarette in the hallways and stuff the butt out in the little sand boxes before entering the theater. The passageways were blue with smoke, then we emerged into the dark, cool, air-conditioned theater.

I can't tell you why, but when our family went to the movies, we always went to the hallway on the left and sat in the plush loge seats that made up the first four rows of the mezzanine. I clearly recall that my dad said, "Four loge," when he bought the tickets. I noticed the seats down below and above us were different—green cloth with thinner cushions, —not plush beige material, but it wasn't until I was in high school and paying for my own tickets that I realized Dad always splurged for the best seats. When

I figured that out, I was a little proud of him.

Three things stuck with me about entering that theater. It was cool (air conditioning in the desert), it was big (a vast space for the light to be projected), and it was dark (it took time for my eyes to adjust). I was leaving the outside world behind, the heat and relentless sunshine of the desert disappeared. I had escaped. It felt safe. I am not sure why. Maybe it was the fact that Mom would take me and my friends to the Saturday matinee (fifty cents in hand) and leave us there alone and would dependably be back at an appointed hour. Mom would never leave us someplace unsafe. As children, we never add up all the hours our parents spend waiting for us in cars, hallways, or home staring at the clock.

I grew up in a world of childhood independence. No directions, no play dates; we were told to 'go play.' We ran or rode our bikes off in all directions to destinations unknown. Soon there were minibikes and BB guns. No supervision, just a deadline to be home. North Indio was a long Stingray bike ride from downtown and the Yellowmart sporting goods store, with its army surplus, that held us in its thrall, but the theater seemed an explicitly adult place where we were allowed to be on our own.

It was at the Aladdin Theater, sitting with my parents, that I decided I hated musicals. I think it must have been Mom who chose the musical movies. I remember Elvis, *Seven Brides for Seven Brothers,* and *Oklahoma*. It always felt to me like they kept interrupting the story to break out in song and dance. I was there for the stories and didn't understand why anyone would suddenly start singing in the middle of a conversation. That never happened in real life. No one I knew suddenly started dancing. It didn't make any sense. At the first note, I sat there glumly waiting for the music to end so the people on the screen would get back to the story. I have never recovered from this silly version of childhood trauma. It is the rare musical of any sort that can hold my attention. I think the only musical, on stage or in a movie theater, that I went to intentionally was the *Rocky Horror Picture Show*. But even then, happily stoned, I shifted in my seat when the songs went on too long.

I had seen the movie posters for the Ray Harryhausen stop animation classic, *Jason and the Argonauts*. I so wanted to see that movie, but it didn't play at a matinee and Mom wanted no part of it. It was a big deal when Dad said he would take me, just the two of us. My brother, he said, was too young for that movie. My dad worked sixty to seventy hours a week. Six and sometimes seven days. I don't think I had ever been to a movie with him alone. Suddenly, this movie, that night with my dad, became the biggest of deals in my little boy life. We got our snacks and settled into the loge seats. The movie absorbed me. The almost stick figure monsters dancing in their Harryhausen jerky way seemed more real than any monsters I had ever seen. I pushed into my seat, away from the screen and in the darkness, looked up at my dad's face illuminated by the light from the screen. I could feel it coming. My nervous child stomach began to ball up tight. I knew this feeling. It happened in the middle of the night when the terrors came and when I didn't want to do something. It was my nervous warning system. *Not now*, I thought, *not this movie. Not with my dad*. But the sensations began to overwhelm me. Finally, I had to say it. I tugged my dad's sleeve, holding my stomach with my other hand, "My stomach hurts … bad."

I know my dad had seen this happen before. He was always one to see if I could simply recover and carry on. He took my hand and took me to the now smoke-free hallway on the other side of the theater, where the men's room was located. I kept looking at the screen as he led me out. I was desperate to see what was going to happen next. He took me to the restroom. Nothing happened, but I didn't feel better. He tried to help me wait it out, but now I was even more upset that I wasn't seeing the movie. My little emotions snowballed. Finally, Dad gave in. I was crying and he told me we would come back and see it again. I don't think I took that for truth as these things with my dad happened so rarely, but it was enough of a reassurance for me to leave. I never saw the rest of that movie. Decades later, I watched that movie on my laptop. "It's kind of scary," I thought, "No wonder I was afraid."

Movies, cars, and high school all ran together. In the 70s, now acknowledged as perhaps the greatest decade of American film making, I saw movies like *The Godfather* and *Chinatown* at the Aladdin. This is when I began what I will call 'the lean in.' Movies started to engage my mind and literally pull me closer to the screen. I would lean forward, rest my elbows on my legs, and poke my head forward like a bird stretching for a berry on a branch. I began to see movies as films and moved beyond plot to see them as a collection of decisions by a team of people. Light, dark, action, dialogue, silence. A new question kept popping into my head, "How did they do that?"

A car put me in motion to new movie theaters, especially one in Palm Springs called The Camelot. Theaters of a time had fanciful, dreamy names. This one was meant to conjure up the Kennedy clan. This new movie palace had a huge, wraparound 70mm screen and surround sound. We marveled at all the speakers hanging on the walls above and behind us. Before, the sound only came from the screen.

Now, the sound was everywhere for movies like *Jaws* and *The Exorcist*. Like a childhood toy, my much-loved Aladdin now seemed a little shabby and old.

There have been two entertainment constants in my life: live music and movies. But by a wide margin a trip to a theater is the winner. When in the throes of my panic disorder, even when I was mostly agoraphobic and barely left my home, the one place I could still find a break from myself, the place where I could feel safe, was a movie theater. I would head out, find a place to park my car close for a quick escape I never really needed, and settled into a seat, popcorn in hand. My seat was always on the aisle and the first thing I would do, still do, was scan the room for the exits. That mental inventory done, I could mostly relax and enjoy the film. Well, except when a wave of panic would roll over me and I would once again see if the exits were still there.

When I arrived in Portland, with little cash in my pockets, I set a goal to see at least one movie in every theater in the city. In the 80s, movie theaters were in transition. The great movie houses of the past were on their last legs. Too large to fill every night, lacking the embrace of the surrounding parking lots of the multi-screen suburban theaters, the grand dames of the past were about to be torn down. One by one, I visited them all. I arrived early so I could spend time in the lobby, walk up to the balconies, and down to the screens. In each location, I paused, looked up, down, and around to see the remnants of former grandness. There were the fake balconies on some high walls, terra cotta frills, and faded paintings of knights, Egyptian palaces, and Hollywood heroes. I imagined what it must have been like to come to these wide-open rooms in their prime, the excitement, the projected light clearly outlined all the way to the screen in blue cigarette smoke and uniformed ushers roaming about, flashlights in hand. Some of the large theaters had balconies that had been walled off to create a second, upstairs screen, a formula to extend the life of the palace. I would stand at the front of the house and stare at the new wall above my head. It was as if part of the space had been amputated to save the body. An ugly scar.

One night, I went to the Broadway Theater in downtown Portland. It was the last movie ever in that theater on the street that shared its name. The swooping neon Broadway on the outside had scattered dark gaps. Other neon was faded, feebly blinking on and off. The carpet in the lobby was red, thin, and stained. Everywhere I looked were signs that at some point people had given up. The smell of popcorn couldn't hide the odor of decay. Once in my seat, it was hard to ignore the smell of mold and urine. Rats walked with impunity down the aisle as I shared the cavernous space with a handful of other humans. Water dripped from expanding stains in the ceiling. It was cold. I guess they had decided to save a last few dollars on electricity. I don't remember the movie but that is not why I was there, not really. I was there to imagine what it had been.

About the same time the palaces were collapsing, small neighborhood theaters began to play foreign language movies. I went to school on movies I had missed when I was younger and mastered the split eyeball art of reading subtitles and watching the actors at the same time. I joined a cadre of film geeks who didn't reflexively say no when the movie wasn't in English, though I will admit I have to be in the right frame of mind to give up the ease of my own language.

A couple of the grand movie houses in my town have been saved and restored by the always perfect combination of beer and pizza. Smaller neighborhood theaters, some almost 100 years old, discovered the same formula and are thriving. I only go to what I call 'mega whopper plexs' in the suburbs by necessity. The great theater preservation miracle of the twentieth century was the proliferation of micro brewed ales, a symbiosis no one could have anticipated.

I am of an age where I need to attend funerals and memorial services too often. It's always best to be the attendee and not the honored at such affairs. Sitting in churches and assorted halls, in grief and celebration, I have begun to ponder what sort of event my own passing would inflict on those who felt they needed to grieve collectively. I have seen the remains of friends used in rituals they never would have approved. For the comfort of the living, robed celebrants engaged in what mostly seemed pointless soul harvesting. I guess it gave others comfort and the dead don't complain, but I had to swallow my disgust to do and say all the right things. I also pondered what I thought was my sacred space. In those moments, I wished I was in a movie theater, a big, cool and safe place.

My perfect ritual would be a double feature. This is a tradition that has disappeared in modern times. When we go to the movie, we go to *a* movie. But there was a time when people went to 'the movies.' I got to see the very tail end of the newsreels. There was a time when the only way to *see* what was happening in the world was to go to the movies. To lighten the mood, the news was followed with a couple of cartoons followed by the first feature. The first movie was often a table setter, a triviality before the main attraction. That is where we harvest B movies for late night festivals. I think that drive-ins, in an effort to offer value, sell more popcorn, and stay alive, were the last place to regularly see a double feature. In the time of the great movie palaces, between the two movies people went to the restroom, smoked, and loaded up on more snacks. A night at the theater was a full event. It was a time of well cultivated long attention spans.

At my final movie night, I want my first feature to have subtitles. There is a rare Japanese movie called *Afterlife*. While I don't subscribe to the concept of an afterlife, that really isn't what the movie is about. Weaving in little clips of real people talking about loss, it resolves as a story about how one finds the people they love. When it comes to grief, even the most hardened need a good cry. That movie will do the trick. After reloading with beer, pizza, and candy, the second feature is pure joy. I first saw *Stop Making Sense*, Johnathan Demme's film of a live Talking Heads concert, in a small movie palace with a balcony. From the second song, people could not resist getting up and dancing in the aisles. I have seen it many times and while people didn't dance, I always see those first dancers in my head. That seems about right. Leave them dancing.

We each come to our own holy places in different ways. Once there, the experience is universal. Emotions resonate like the strings on a strummed guitar. Joy, sadness, calm, relief, deep thought, and no thought. And sometimes, like a stroked chord, it all comes together as a chill or sensation of warmth that works its way down from your face to your toes. My place is a movie theater. I wonder what is playing tonight.

HAND

———————————

MY WIFE AND I flew down on my birthday. The funeral was the next morning.

Few things are as consistently lovely as the Southern California weather in November. We had to be at the staging area at exactly 11:31 AM. Not 11:30 … 11:31. National cemeteries are both beautiful and run with military precision. Mom was the wife of a veteran so has the honor of resting among Dad's peers and their spouses. It had taken weeks to secure this service time. The escalating pace of the passing of the Greatest Generation makes a national cemetery a busy place.

The current Blackwoods have a tenuous relationship with our various religions. There would be no church service, just a small commitment ceremony in one of the many concrete gathering places scattered around the cemetery. Mom wanted it that way.

I come from a long line of storytellers. Hillbilly roots easily blend the taciturn and talkative. Long ago, I decided that we are all our collection of stories. In the weeks between my mother's passing and the family gathering, four different stories about my mom played in rotation in my head. In the shower, as I meditated, sitting at stop lights, and every night as I tried to sleep, I told those stories to myself. Honing them became the quiet work of each day. I never wrote them out completely. I stuck to a few prompts on a piece of paper. What I said I had tightly installed in my synapses.

Two days before we departed, I threw out one of the stories. Three was all I needed. I wanted to help people laugh. Describe my folks as a couple. Give people an intimate picture of my relationship with my mom.

Dad was very much the paternal master of the day. His steadfastness in meeting my mom's wishes and embodying his deep love were our guiding light. I will admit that as I sat there looking at the polished wooden coffin my brother and I had helped roll into place, I had a hard time following Dad's words. My brother had typed the pages for Dad's script, but what was most striking was how he broke from that reassuring script to tell the story of his great grandson running to meet him the day before. This storytelling thing is deep in the genes.

He turned to me. I stood next to the coffin. I felt disoriented as I was not sure if I was next to Mom's head or feet. It's simply a problem that had never crossed my mind before. My hands were unsteady, so I laid my crib sheet on the coffin. Strange, that. First, I thanked my dad and brother for the loving care they provided for years of Mom's descent into dementia. I was the distant one and barely got to be in that loving and awful circle. Then the stories came. In the telling I realized I was calm. I watched people, especially my nieces, laugh and well up as I spoke. One of the most unnatural things I have ever done felt natural. It didn't make sense. I easily stayed up on that wave.

The last story was tough to start.

My mother called me her space boy. I was born at the right time to grow up with the American space program. I knew everything a kid could know about the Mercury, Gemini, and Apollo space capsules. I had a poster of a Saturn 5 rocket, the one that would take us to the moon, on my bedroom wall. Besides Willie Mays, my other childhood hero was Ed White, the first man to walk in space. I can still touch sadness thinking about him dying in a flash, pure oxygen fueled fire on the pad in Apollo One.

Mom was right there with me about space and the race to the moon. It was this shared love that gave us a ritual … our ritual.

The rockets mostly launched in the early morning from Cape Canaveral in Florida. On launch days, it was still dark on the west coast. Mom would wake me, and we would turn on our black and white TV to watch the launch. For me, this experience always smelled like my mom's fresh brewed Yuban coffee.

We'd sit next to each other on the couch and hang on every minute of the countdown. I dreaded halts to the count as I still had to go to school, launch or not. Then the NASA launch control announcer would count down from ten. Mom always stood leaning toward the TV, hands tensely balled in front of her.

Lift off! The bright light from the rockets blurred the television image. Then it happened. She would say, "Go! … Go! … Go!…Go … !" I would join her in the chant. She often made this high pitched sound, like the sound of joy you hear when girls gather on a playground. We chanted until the rocket became a small white dot on the TV screen.

When I told that part of the story, I first told everyone what I had felt for the last years of my mom's decline with dementia. For me, it felt like she was trapped here on earth and that now she was free. As I told the rocket story, I wanted to say the word "Go" three times. Without thinking, I slapped my hand on the casket with the first "Go."

Suddenly, I was brought back to earth by the loud sound of my wedding ring hitting the casket. I was shocked by the sound. Solid. Metal on wood. I turned to look at my hand on the casket like a foreign body was making that noise. *Did I do that?*

I tried to cup my fingers for the second "Go." Still, that jarring sound. I looked up at everyone, wondering, *Are you hearing that?*

Don't do that again, I thought. I almost didn't but in the speed of a racing mind I knew I had no choice. *No. Go ahead. This is what this is. That is your hand. This is Mom's coffin.* I slapped the wood one more time and finished what I had come there to do.

ANGER

TEMPER IS A TWO-FACED WORD. I have a temper. I was raised amongst people with tempers. Once my dad, angry, seeking release and not wanting to harm me, put his fist through the wall of my teenager bedroom. He got my attention. I saw my mom, angry over Dad carelessly hacking away at her much-loved carnations, pull up every flower in the bed and toss them into the yard screaming, red faced, out of control. Their anger energy was directed at things, not people. Temper, the hair trigger threat of violence, is a frightening thing to witness and experience in one's self.

The verb form temper is often a good thing. By heating and cooling steel, it becomes both harder and more elastic, capable of keeping an edge and resisting repeated punishment. When actions are tempered by wisdom, outcomes can improve. Tempering can be the process of calming and providing context. It is a vital part of relationships and building community. I am sure that my ability to calm others and inject humor into tense situations is the product of the child not wanting to see my parents' anger explode in my direction. My mind and heart were tempered by anger. It is one of the sources of my resilience.

Anger is one way I protect myself in the world. As a child there was a game we played called 'Burn.' Whoever could say something that belittled someone, or put them in their place, was rewarded with the exclamation, "What a burn!" There was a surprising lack of malice in the game. It was mostly verbal jousting with a small reward for one-upmanship. Tall, gaunt, and skinny, with no strength or reflexes to speak of, I was the last one picked for every team on the playground. What I learned about the physical world was that it was a place of shame and bullying. However, I had one edge, a quick mind for witty invective. I found my power in words and the ability to manipulate them. For me, the game was easy and fun and other people laughed at my wit or cowered when I unleashed it.

This innate skill turned into the ability to debate almost any topic. I have a rolodex memory. (Now there's a word that dates me. There used to be a spinning card filing system on every professional desk that contained all of one's contacts. The common line was that if you got fired, "Take your Rolodex.") Now, I suppose you would say I have a relational database memory. Most of what I read and hear gets filed away. I genuinely don't know what I know until someone mentions a topic, then the information pops into my head. I actually see the pages or websites where I originally read what I suddenly remember. My urge to share what I once again know, exciting to me, can annoy others in the most uber-nerdy way. Wit plus memory made me a powerful debater.

Here's the problem with only having a quick tongue to protect yourself. With each received insult or shove or punch, my body stores an unclaimed reaction. Physical bullies are rarely restrained by the rapid-fire insult. At moments where I faced actual physical danger, I was also smart enough to know that opening my mouth would likely compound the abuse and humiliation I knew was coming next. My psyche became a collection of unresolved violence, punches not thrown, kicks not unleashed, fleet footed escapes not made. I lived in an internal world of, "I wish I could have …" For souls like me, there is a price to be paid for all that unresolved anger. My gene pool bequeathed me a tightly wound nervous system that left me with a variety of anxiety disorders. Like a puppy chasing his tail, I spun myself in a tight circle of unresolved anger. Anxiety and anger fused as a constant background hum in my mind.

Simmering anger can manifest itself in curious ways. I love to be around smart people who want to discuss any topic. Like a Border Collie who sees a squirrel, I instantly perk up and feel a rush of excitement. I have to consciously tell myself, hold back, listen, let other people speak. I am better at that now but when my blood is up, I can barely restrain myself. I love to challenge and be challenged. A natural contrarian, I am always looking to puncture conventional wisdom. As I engage, my physical aspect changes. I lean forward, and slowly, imperceptibly to me, the volume of my voice raises. Both anxiety and anger become very confusing in the face of simple excitement. The physical sensations, especially early on, are essentially the same. I often don't know which pathology will manifest first. I am most fearful of the anxiety, less so with anger, and am willing to let the anger creep forward a little more, as it seems more controllable.

Internally, I am riding a wave of happiness. I rarely bare malice in my arguments but the deeper into the discussion, the more the outside world begins to interpret my engagement as aggression. I am unaware. Many of my foils, in these moments, are also powerful verbal and intellectual jousters ready for a little rough and tumble. They understand we are putting ideas on the table and taking baseball bats to them. But I have trouble tracking who is comfortable and who isn't. I may feel like I am holding back but have already crossed a line I can't see. Some folks back away … all the way away … and choose not to engage me at all.

When wit is also one's ultimate defense the internal dialogue can be a little scary. If there was an imaginary outward manifestation of my internal dialogue, it would look like a guy walking around with his hands up, arms coiled, fists tight. You would see that guy and ask, "Why does he always look like he is ready for a fight?" In my mind, that is exactly the posture I maintain. I live with a little fear of the world all the time. While I manage that fear every day, there is a deeper truth about my lifelong anxiety. I am always a little angry at the reality that I am always a little afraid. Like that invisible tension you feel when you play with two magnets and flip one to its opposite poll, for me the magnets of fear and anger are always tumbling, sometimes sticking together, other times repelling each other.

A curious gift of this constant readiness of my finely tuned fight or flight, is a keen awareness of the world around me. I watch people closely. The fear side of me does a quick assessment: friend or foe. The anger part of me is cataloging intellectual and emotion chinks in other people's armor. It happens so automatically, so quickly, that my doing it rarely registers consciously. This is the unprompted calculation of how I could marshal my mind to defend myself. I am quickly loading arrows in my mind's quiver. From vulnerable and friendly, to biting and hostile, I choose from an array of words and phrases. At the angry end of the scale is the phrase or sentence that could emotionally devastate the person in front of me. At the ready, as I am talking, discussing, arguing, I know what the ultimate weapon will be. It is both troubling and powerful to know that in my vulnerability I can defend myself in an instant. Like a nuke in a missile silo in Nebraska, I take reassurance that the weapon exists, and while I genuinely hope never to deploy it, I sometimes have a *Dr. Strangelove* fantasy about the effect if I did.

It is a dark art, this ability to harm with a word. A quick, unseen rapier cut. The evil side of our nature is a temptation. We all have it but rarely want to acknowledge what we are capable of in an instant. The villain in the play both repels and intrigues us. Some of the greatest characters in literature are explorations of contained, carefully marshaled evil. We fear that power in anyone who has no restraints, the sociopath. I don't think I am unique. Maybe my little manifestation of evil is different, but history tells us that anyone is capable of the most heinous acts given the right threat and given the perfect justification of enough hate or fear or love.

When I have had actual enemies, bullies, I engage in a reverie, an internal dialogue with that person where I actually deploy my verbal nuke. I suppose everyone has a variation of a revenge fantasy. Having the thought decreases the inner tension and lets me blow off steam and remind myself that I am not that person ... not really. How many movies or books have your seen where the plot involves acting or not acting on a revenge fantasy. In movies, sometimes the portrayal of the revenge fantasy is used as a tension relieving funny aside, a madcap adventure. But because I am always a little afraid, there is seldom anything humorous about my little fantasies. I have learned let go of them, but each one seems like a way to survive in a dangerous world.

I'm sure that my not understanding when I am coming on too strong with someone is, in part, because I have anticipated my worst. I have the worst case in my head. I am ready. So, perversely, any argument I make that doesn't 'go there' seems reasonable. It feels like I am in control. I have made a rational choice. My wife sometimes warns me, "Jim, don't weaponize your intellect." Cold comfort to anyone I have frightened or offended.

I know my anger triggers. Injustice hovers at the top of list. If I see someone, or some creature, being treated unjustly, ticking anger becomes rage. Naturally, this is especially the case with the abuse of children. The vulnerability of a child frightens me because of its deep traumatic resonance in my own life. With no little irony, caring for such children is my wife's profession. In all our time together, we have had a simple rule. She can't tell me about what happened to the kids she sees at work. When some incident does leak into our conversation, I can only a think about swift, physical vengeance. There is no middle, healing ground, just the beast within me. My acute awareness contains it.

While honorable behavior can quickly bring me to tears, dishonorable acts can easily fuel my ire. Only a few times have I confronted injustice directly, but every time I pay a physical price. Hot in the moment, soon after I am overwhelmed by the adrenaline and become a shaking, shivering mess. I have the courage to face down evil but maybe not the nervous system for the job. Released anger modulates back to anxiety, my eternal internal twins.

In the end, I am most often angry at myself. Start with perfectionism. Like many people, I suffered from imposter syndrome. In my work, at school, in my interactions with other people, I set for myself impossible standards. When I have been at the top of my game professionally, I mostly saw the flaws and kept looking around to see if anyone else has noticed that I was faking it. With time and the study of Zen Buddhism, I taught myself to slow down, leave my busy mind, and try to be in the moment. I have constructed little rituals of presence. *Look around. See the faces. Where am I? What building am in? Am I breathing?* I try to leave my internal world of self-judgment to make a tangible, irrefutable connection with the physical world of the moment. I often reach up and touch the little sitting Buddha charm on a necklace under my shirt. In turn, these rituals allow me to connect with people.

I am not so foolish as to believe that after all this time I will suddenly let go of my anger. It is as much me as my boney elbows. Consciousness is control. I have created the rattling pot lid that lets steam escape, releasing my worst impulses in small ways. Cut me off in traffic? "Fuck off!" I say to my windshield. I talk back to televisions and yell encouragement at ballgames. (Yeah, it's the yelling alone that does the trick. It doesn't have to be negative.) I write myself into submission in my journal or slam out 1,000-word essays to the internet. Most importantly, I get regular doses of loud, live music where the bass notes rattle my chest. My wife knows the signs and reminds me, "You really need to go see a show." I drive my car in challenging ways on lonely back roads forcing all my attention to the road and movement. Sizzle. Hiss. The relief valve opens and closes.

There is a deep irony in my self-awareness of the turmoil that lies right beneath my surface. In life, especially in my careers, I am often seen as the calmest one in the room. I am the steady hand, the sea anchor in the storm. When other people are angry or sad or confused, I can be there with them and not get caught up in their emotions. Acting calm creates calm. I deprive the sensations pulsing inside me. I have worked hard to create the ability to detach from what is happening in front of me. I am now most naturally an observer and have taught myself to call on that skill on demand. People who are chronically anxious mask the outward manifestation of their inner lives with projected calm. It is a skill that helps us hide. What I hide is not only anxiety but anger.

I have always been on the lookout for people who know how to manage and use their anger in ways that don't harm others. They don't deny the power of the emotion; they channel it. I sometime see this ability in athletes, especially baseball pitchers. Pitching at the highest level is impossibly hard. The pitcher must master and then repeat an intricate set of physical motions that result in a ball being located exactly where they want it sixty-six feet, six-inches away. There are many pitchers with the physical skill to achieve that, but there are rare few who master their minds. Standing alone on the mound between pitches, there is too much time to think. Careers have ended not because of a lack of physical skills but because of an unstoppable collection of the wrong thoughts.

My icons do something wonderful; they contain and

harness anger. Hall of Fame baseball pitchers, like Randy Johnson and Bob Gibson, were feared for the anger and fierceness they brought onto the field with them every time they pitched. They were known to have a chip on their shoulders and pitch angry. Before the game, they went into a zone and marshalled their anger. No teammate dared talk to them. On the mound, they glowered and kicked dirt, argued calls with umpires, and stared in to intimidate hitters. Now and again, they threw something hard, fast, and inside to push a cocky batter from the plate. What those pitchers did was not an act. They felt real emotion and used the heat of anger to turn up their adrenaline and focus. A little rage goes a long way when you need motivation to do the hard things. But here's the thing; once they walked off the mound at the end of the game, they let go of their anger. I recall listening to them talk after the game. Their real voices were quiet, calm, and even shy.

Like those pitchers, I like to think I have arrived in a place where I know how to marshal my anger. I use it to motivate me to do hard things, and when I see anger in others, I understand what they are feeling and how to defuse it. While I don't always succeed and the impulse sometimes bleeds across the line, I have also mastered the art of the heartfelt apology and willingness to reconsider. Anger also taught me humility, a gift I may have not achieved any other way.

INSIDER

POLITICS IS A WORLD OF SECRETS. For about a decade, I was part of those secrets. I left a long career in information systems to complete a dream and work in politics and public policy. The transition was improbable, if not impossible, but with hard work, a patient wife, and some luck, I did it. I became a political advisor and senior policy director for a city commissioner. I was an insider, a guy who knew secrets. Years away from that world, my secrets are mostly known now, except one. I can count on my hands the people who know the truth of this story. I was instrumental in the removal of the highest non-elected official in my city, the Chief Administrative Officer (CAO). At the time, many people were sure how his departure came about. They were wrong.

I came to City Hall with a breadth of experience in the corporate world. I had been with the same multi-billion-dollar public company for over two decades. Among the staffs of the five elected officials on city council I was an oddity. In liberal Portland, happening upon a socially liberal, fiscally conservative moderate was like seeing an orange whale in the Arctic. Still, there I was, and damn happy about it. I was that anonymous soul you see walking behind an elected official or standing in the back of the room staring at their phone.

For all of this to make sense, I need to explain Portland's curious and archaic form of city government. There are four commissioners and a mayor, all elected city-wide, no districts. There is no city manager. The mayor has two powers, handing out the city bureaus to commissioners to manage and presenting the city's budget for approval by the full city council. It's an awful system where rank amateurs run billion-dollar bureaus. A former nurse in charge of parks. A real estate guy in charge of the police bureau. A bookstore owner running the department of transportation. Even more insane, there is a tradition that commissioners don't get into the bureau business of other commissioners and the mayor, even in the face of utter mismanagement. It's a horse with five heads, each looking in a different direction. Giddy up! However, there is one essential rule: on a council of five, there is a rule of three. Three votes can do almost anything. Previous mayors have had careers scuttled because they could not count to three.

With the right kind of elected official, being a staffer can be powerful. You are the intersection of decision making, acting as a gatekeeper to the raw information of power. On good days, I was a sounding board for decisions because I had a boss eager for diverse opinions. My favorite part of my pubic service was the countless hours I spent behind closed doors discussing policy, politics, and messaging with my boss and other senior staff. I know some people resent that so much that happens in politics occurs out of sight. I can't think of any other way it could happen. That is exactly why we live in a republic with elected representatives. By definition, the public has chosen to outsource the sausage making.

The mayor's portfolio includes the financial apparatus of the city. That makes sense given his responsibility for the budget. The one official with a city-wide view, the person who coordinates all of the city's financial functions, is the CAO. Below him is the Chief Financial Officer (CFO). In my corporate world there is a troika of power at the top of corporations: CEO (Chief Executive Officer), CFO, and Chief Technology Officer (CTO).

One day, the mayor announced that to save money, he had fired the city's CFO. Word was there had been friction between the CAO and CFO, so there may have been a little political payback, but the part that set off my personal alarm bell was that the mayor was not going to replace the CFO. In a city that had a multi-billion-dollar public portfolio, that function was going to happen by committee. This seemed crazy to me. How could that possibly work? To my chagrin, while there was a little grousing from the city commissioners, the leaders seemed to be falling into the tradition of no one messing with the mayor's portfolio. I registered my concern with my boss, but he was a former lawyer, with no experience in large financial entities. I quickly saw that I could rant and wave my arms all I wanted but he wasn't going to move. I had learned long before that when someone can't hear you, no matter how right you may be, get an expert to deliver the same message. In the corporate world, consulting is a billion-dollar industry of strangers telling powerful people what their own employees had been saying for years.

In my old career, my teams managed business critical computing platforms. It was rare that our work was not being audited by both inside and outside auditors. Auditors are annoying creatures. Inevitably, they are wonky, bureaucratic, and more than a little aware of their power while trying to be your momentary friend. I resisted them until I figured it out. Audit reports, with the right information in them, were the keys to the cash register. Things I had advocated for that had languished out of reach suddenly became a priority if an auditor said it. With that in mind, I recalled a meeting I once had with the city's outside financial auditor. I had my man.

When I called Rick, my soon-to-be new best political friend, the head outside auditor, I switched from city guy to corporate guy. We talked oversight and independent financial advice and best practices. Auditors love to talk about best practices. It's like they have an undying loyalty to a childhood football team, The Fighting Best Practices. I brought our conversation to the city no longer having a CFO. It's funny to me now, but as a political insider, there are often parts of phone conversations where the person on the other end of the line slows down, lowers his voice, and becomes slightly conspiratorial. I loved it when that happened because now we had entered a small world of shared interests. Turns out, and I knew this all along, our chief financial auditor was both offended and deeply concerned the city no longer had a CFO. He was relieved that someone else noticed. Auditors are powerless without patrons.

I had to keep everything I was doing very quiet as I was now crossing political power boundaries. Kind of a thrill actually, as I have never been one to respect boundaries. Too much punk rock in my soul. In a series of phone calls and a meeting, I asked Rick to assume a new role, that of educator. I needed him to make the case to my commissioner that removing a CFO from the city was a grievous error. Generally, any outsider always coveted one-on-one time with the commissioner in his office. In many ways, providing that access was one of my most powerful tools. Once in with the commissioner, knowing their time was precious, people would always bring their A game. From my observer's chair, I barely said a word. My boss had a remarkable ability to narrow into an issue and ask cogent questions. Halfway through, I saw he got it. He told me that with a silent look and raised eyebrow. More importantly, as someone who believed deeply in transparency and competence in government, it was clear he was now both offended and an advocate. We were on our way.

There were more meetings. God only knows how many calls my boss made on his ubiquitous cell phone. But very quickly, I was working with a deputy city attorney to draft a new law that recreated the office of CFO and prescribed new duties and obligations as an independent financial advisor to all of city council. About the same time, I began to put out feelers with my staff counterparts in two of the other commissioner's offices.

There is a Starbucks right across the street from Portland City Hall. I would wager as much city business gets done there as in any conference room. The rhetorical tap dance between staff counterparts was an almost prescribed game. We could be informal, even friendly, talk about our lives and gossip a bit about 'the building' as we called City Hall. Like talking to reporters, these conversations were a fun sort of three-dimensional chess game based on a few questions. *What do I know that I want you to know? What do you want to know that I can't reveal? How much do we share now and what gets shared later? What is our body language telling each other? I know neither of us can commit on behalf of our bosses, but what hints can we hand back and forth? Most importantly, do each of us have the message we are going to bring back to our bosses?* It was a little exhausting, doing that all day, but it was also a rush. Time would flash by during such conversations. I suppose the caffeine helped.

Now I had a draft law and we were looking for the all-powerful three votes. Generally, elected members had walk-in privileges in each other's offices. If one of them showed up and asked for a word with the commissioner, whatever was happening stopped. All of them had insane daily schedules so they were pretty good about making time for each other. One oddity of the form of government is that is against the law for three members to be in the same place at a time. That was legally a quorum and subject to Oregon's strict public meeting laws. I am not kidding. If it happened in a public setting, everything they said had to be recorded. Mostly it meant that negotiations between them became a game of telephone, one pairing after another.

There is a ritual to two council members meeting. Each had a staff member with them, but we were merely notetaking wallpaper. As an introvert, I loved the permission to just observe. Once he had his brief, my lawyerly boss was charming and persuasive. I marveled at his fluency in an issue that he only knew about because one day I got angry. For a staffer, this was as good as it gets, having your idea come to life in the hands of someone who can make it a reality. I never got over the buzz of that dynamic.

Now we had our three votes. My inclination at that

point was to show our three and go. Screw the mayor and the other commissioners. They could get onboard or not, who cares. I was the kind of political nerd who studied the masters: Paul Begalia and James Carvelle from the Clinton campaign; David Plouffe and David Axlerod from Obama's genius campaigns, and especially, the Bush guru, Karl Rove. My political operative self could divorce political skill from policy positions. Rove's clarity, wonkiness, and simple ruthlessness was a wonder to behold. Once, on a campaign, I was accused by the opposition of being the evil Karl Rove-like Republican operative. I loved it. But that wasn't my boss. He was always looking for compromise and accommodation. He always tried to get all five votes and his preference was my duty.

Not everyone was like my boss. Other members filed their laws and resolutions with no notice and they quietly showed up on the calendar on Friday mornings. That wasn't our way. My boss always consulted his peers.

I had everything ready when he said, "Take it up to the mayor's chief of staff and let them respond."

"On my way," I said. *Fuck her*, I thought.

A few weeks before, in a large meeting, I had tried to do my boss's bidding and be accommodating. She had taken relish in issuing a public beat down. I didn't forget. So, I did what my boss asked and went up to her office, poked my head in the door, and said, "Have a moment to look at something from my commissioner?" She looked annoyed and motioned me to her desk.

I tossed the one-page draft in front of her and cheerily said, "The commissioner would like to give the mayor an opportunity to respond."

She was reading. Her head came back slightly and she

turned toward me.

"What the hell is this!"

I said, "So we are clear. We have three votes and are ready to file, but it's Nick's preference to work with the mayor." I smiled, "We will wait to hear from you." In my head, *Yeah, fuck with me again … just try it.*

Later that same day, the mayor, big smile, strolled into our office for a quick one-on-one meeting with the commissioner. He was angry and was stalling for time. He had ordered the CAO to come to us after the weekend to explain how the CFO by committee would work. My boss said he'd listen.

I am pretty good at reading people in a conference room. I had been in meetings with the CAO many times. What was clear about him was that his greatest skill was surrounding himself with smart people. He never came to a meeting without them. He depended on their answers and expertise and then swooped in to repeat what they said and take credit. Throughout my career I had seen those sorts of charlatans in action. That morning he met with the commissioner and me alone. He had three copies of something he had prepared over the weekend. He handed them out and began to explain. It was immediately clear that what was most important to him was maintaining his control and power. The document was, at best, amateurish and completely self-serving. At one point, my boss turned away from him and to me with widened eyes, the sign for WTF. After the meeting my commissioner called the mayor, told him he wasn't buying what the CAO was selling. By the end of the day, the mayor announced that he was recruiting a new CFO. He didn't want the embarrassment of a council session on our new law. Game over … we had prevailed … except ….

Now my life got weird. Our draft law became public. As the author, I was quoted in one of the newspaper stories. The next day I got a furtive call from a high ranking financial official who worked for the CAO. She wanted to meet me. I said sure. "But not here," she said.

I first saw the movie *All The President's Men* in a small, old theater in downtown Salem, Oregon. Leaning forward, elbows on my knees, I was absorbed, not just in the story of Watergate, but by the working lives of the reporters. It was the 'Deep Throat' garage scene from that movie that was on my mind as early one morning I parked my Mini Cooper in front of a Starbuck's on the other side of the Willamette River from downtown Portland. I had seen the woman I was meeting testify on city finance issues, but I didn't know her. At least I knew what she looked like. I greeted her, grabbed a hot tea, and spent the next hour listening to her story. She told me she had seen my quotes in the newspaper and thought I was someone who cared about city management and could be trusted. She was clear but also nervous and a little sad. She painted a picture of mismanagement of the city's finances by the CAO. Then, one by one, she shared printed email exchanges with the CAO from a large stack in front of her. There were emails between her and another important woman in her department. As I read them, it was clear that the CAO was both disrespectful to staff and seeking to hide some things from oversight. I ended by reassuring her I would hold her contact with me in strictest confidence and see what I could do. I purposely didn't take any of her papers with me. As a public official, if had them, a reporter could request them.

"Holy shit," I said out loud when I got back to my car.

She had confirmed my general impressions of the CAO and everything was far worse than I thought. We had won the policy fight, but this was something entirely new, more fraught with political problems. I shared what I learned with the commissioner and our chief of staff. In my entire time at City Hall, those were the only two people who knew the entire story. I never told anyone else with whom I worked. With my wife, the circle was four people. It was about to get bigger.

During my time in politics, I very much adopted my commissioner's approach to reporters and recognized that they, too, had an important job to do. I am a lifelong news junkie who loves reporters for what they do. I maintained relationships with reporters across the little Portland media world, especially the two City Hall reporters from the state-wide newspaper, *The Oregonian*. In an archaic oddity, they actually had an office on the ground floor of City Hall. Some days, I made a point of stopping by on the way home to shoot the breeze and answer their questions … off the record. Because, unlike many of the others in the building, I made a point to be approachable and would sometimes give them little bits of insight; our dance of access was a two-way street. I especially enjoyed talking with a reporter who had been a real pain in the ass for my boss several times. He was delightfully cynical and a relentless researcher when he had the bit of a good story between his teeth.

One day I purposely ran into him and said, "Let's have coffee. And let's do it way off campus."

His head cocked, "What?"

"Way off," I said again.

I decided that I was going to make it my business to take down the CAO. I had seen underwhelming people in positions of power all across my professional life. It was pretty common. In my public service, two things were a constant. I believed that, run well, government could be a positive force in people's lives, especially for those who didn't have access to power. Having been a private sector guy for so long, I knew that big corporations were also as inefficient and screwed up as the public sector. Now I was trying to make government run better for people. I suppose it was sort of a calling, why I left my lucrative career. The second great personal truth was that I hated bullies. I lived with the psychological scars of bullying and my response when I saw a bully in action was instant and visceral. Honestly, I always want to punch them in the face. Yeah, that intense. Now I had chance to act on two of my fundamental values. I didn't ever expect I would be in this position, but I wasn't going to waste it.

Using only non-public communication, personal cell phones, nothing in writing, I confirmed from my source, whom I now considered a sort of whistleblower, that she was okay with what I was going to do. I met the reporter blocks from City Hall at an unpopular coffee shop, back of the room.

Sitting down, I said "This is all off the record. Seriously, way off the record."

He perked up and reaffirmed what I said. I then told him the story. Oregon has powerful pubic records laws. I simply told him where to look.

I continued to communicate with the women via home emails and personal cell phone calls. The first story to appear in the press was devastating. I had chosen the right reporter and he now painted a picture of abuse of power, manipulation of city finances, and outright incompetence.

The mayor's office fought back hard against the media. But the accumulating evidence rolled out in story after story as the other news outlets got on the scent. Pressure built. One of the women chose to go public, on the record, handing over more evidence. The mayor had to fire the CAO. My commissioner's only reaction was that based on the evidence he supported the mayor's decision. No one ever learned how it all happened. Well, until now.

These powerful women had taken an awful risk with their careers. Throughout the ordeal I had been in secret communication with them. Sometimes they just wanted to vent. Other times, they asked my advice. From the first, it was clear that they needed to control their own destinies. I was only going to be the vehicle of their desires. From both of them I received touching thank yous for my support. I never shared those with anyone but my wife.

For a moment, I was an insider. I am proud of what I changed, the part that got out in the open. But behind the curtain, I got to do what was right and with no credit and no tracks in the snow for anyone to follow. Somehow, that is even better.

GRIP

IT IS ENTIRELY LIKELY I care too much about a handshake. I come from a time and place and culture where how one's hand was offered and received was deemed a critical indication of the worth of a person. A handshake, or the refusal to offer one's hand, could instantly mark someone, for good or bad, for life. I am not kidding. Beyond the admonition that first impressions are lasting impressions, the way someone shakes my hand can be a deal breaker. No matter how hard I try to keep an open mind about someone I meet for the first time, I have been encoded to overvalue the offered hand. You've been warned.

The handshake violates all other norms of human behavior. Deep in the genetic code, our upright species demands caution when happening upon a stranger. We walk around with enforced personal space bubbles. Hug a friend but keep strangers at arm's length where you can see them from their toes to their nose. That is enough space to parry a thrown fist or duck or run. That little tingle of discomfort you feel when someone is close-talking you is all about the survival of the species. Listen to the tingle.

There is this ritual when two people decide to violate the rational, genetic rules of survival and touch each other. Puncturing the jostling safety zones, we look in each other's eyes, apply a friendly face, and extend our hands toward each other. Carvings, thousands of years old, show people greeting each other with handshakes. Some deep thinkers have speculated the act was a symbol of peace showing that the mostly dominant right hand was not holding a weapon. That makes sense in the pre-gun age. However, this makes my point. The act itself is an indication of safety. *Hey Roman dude, you show me you don't have a knife and I will do the same … okay?* There is more than symbolic power in violating the most natural instinct to 'keep my distance.'

Given the innate deep meaning and lineage of the handshake, I suppose it was only natural for our ever-judging brains to then apply other, more subtle, meanings to the gesture. Having relinquished safety, we shift to the quality of the handshake. Here is where we meet the grip.

I am the soft-handed end of a gene pool of men and women who worked with their hands. The prize for such work was calluses and wicked strong grips. The pride in my family's men's ability to grab onto things like a Gila Monster's bite was immense. No tool was every going to fall from their hands and no day's work was going to result in a blister. The mechanics in my family all prided themselves in the fact that they could reach into a hot engine and grab parts whose heat would have left a mere mortal screaming. Along with the strength and toughness of their hands was that to the common eye, their hands never looked clean. No matter how hard they scrubbed with harsh pumice soap, the lines in their hands were clearly visible as a spider web of minute darkened valleys. If, in doing a job, they got a cut or nick, the work would only stop long enough to shake off the blood, stick the wound under a cold faucet and maybe, or maybe not, apply a quick bandage. Blood would soak out of the bandage as oil and grease soaked in.

These are the powerful hands that taught me the handshake. Over and over again the word firm would be repeated like a meditation mantra.

"Stand up," Dad would say, "and look them in the eye. Let them know you mean it when you shake their hand."

And then, we would practice. I would take his hand and feel its almost inhuman hardness, like the padded paw of a German Shepherd.

"Firmer," he would say. "Good. Like that."

Then, inevitably, he would unleash a bit of the power in his hand, crushing mine. I knew he could break bones if he wanted to, but he stopped short.

"Someday, you will be able to do that."

Next would come the often-repeated tale of how as a little guy all Dad had to do in a fight was to get his hands on the arms of his opponent, tighten his vice on them, and bend them down into submission. The story always came with the illustration of him taking invisible arms, crushing them and pushing them down. Then Dad would smile and laugh to himself.

I was the third generation into our story of grips. I grew up working with my dad's father. Grandad, as to all grandkids, seemed very old but the truth of it was that he was a man in his late 50s, still lithe and strong. When my dad talked about grips, he would sometimes pause, back up a little, shake his head and say, "But your grandad … you still don't want to mess with him." I had seen it. When the young, strong mechanics who worked for him were stopped cold by a frozen bolt on a car, Grandad would step in, seemingly make his hand part of the wrench and give the offending bolt one good tug. Pop, snap, and it would move. Then he would step back, grin with small satisfaction, and hand the tool back to the mechanic and in his soft Arkansas accent say something like, "Okay, you do the rest."

Shaking a woman's hand was, of course, different. By degree, I was taught to never crush a woman's hand but to never 'go limp.' Firm was still a sign of respect in all cases, different if you took a woman's hand. I still do a thousand micro muscle calculations when I shake a woman's hand.

Surviving this ninja school for handshakes left me acutely aware of how I offered my hand and received the same. If a man offered a handshake with a grip beyond traditionally firm, then I was taught to do the same. There is a lot of invisible macho stuff going on in the hands of some men. The too-firm grip is a challenge, a question really, "Who are you?" If you know what was intended, and immediately respond in kind, the hand crusher will let go, strangely reassured that he now knows who you are and respects you. It's a weird thing, I know, but it has happened to me many times. Men are strange.

My judgment begins with the eyes and the offer. Did they stand up to meet me? Are they being perfunctory or did the person bring his eyes to meet mine as our hands met? There is something about the eyes. Maybe it's vestigial to the notion that having proven we don't have weapons in our hands, the next challenge is in the eyes. Friendship.

Hostility. Confusion. Detachment. Curiosity. We have the evolutionary design to quickly size up someone. In minute ways we are always sending and receiving messages. The intimacy of the handshake draws us closer where it is almost impossible to miss signals, unless, of course, you have met a master of deception, the soul who uses the handshake to throw you off the trail. People who are leaders have often risen to their posts by mastering the art of quickly insinuated friendship. If you are not paying close attention, or are in their sphere as a supplicant, you will be fooled.

Those of us with handshake training record first encounters on a scale. The limp, uncaringly offered hand is the bottom of the hierarchy. I admit to almost instantaneously feeling disgust. The only thing worse is the failure to make the gesture. A handshake offered without eye contact engenders suspicion. Eye contact with the hand held too long makes me wonder what you want from me, unless, of course, we are already acquainted or friends. Then the held hand is an act of confirmation, a hint of intimacy. The same long hold with a woman is often a confirmation of intimacy—intellectual, emotional, or physical. A handshake can also indicate desire, if not lust. The touch and eyes show the way. When we choose to puncture our safety bubbles and invoke the power of touch, the implications can cascade.

The first impression of a handshake can become a hill for someone else to climb or an instant sensation of standing on level ground. It's a dangerous thing, this reliance on the handshake, the grip, as a marker of value in someone I meet. I have been completely wrong about the person in the long run. But more often than not, what I learned in seconds is confirmed over time. Or did the handshake create my frame and I simply filled in the blanks?

In my youth, I rode a bus across the border to Mexico on a church mission trip. Standing at the front of the bus as we chugged south, the preacher instructed us to shake the hand of everyone if they offered it, especially the dirty, sticky hands of every little child. To not reciprocate any offered handshake would be considered an insult. I understood. But as I looked at the preacher, I recalled the mushy, pink sweating hand that I shook in the foyer exiting Sunday morning services. There was no way I would ever trust that guy. Not with that grip.

AMNESIA

I ALMOST NEVER REMEMBER what I have written. Hours and hours at a keyboard, then marking up hardcopy with my mechanical pencil, endlessly rewriting and when it is done, perhaps only a few weeks later, I read it again and can't recall writing it. I look at the words and think, *Oh, that's a clever sentence. What? Well, that doesn't work.* I critique the writing as if I had picked up a pile of papers on the street and began thumbing my way through them.

There is an otherness to writing. I rarely know what is going to appear on the screen as I am doing it, sometimes startled by the turn of a phrase. First drafts are a mystery to me. Some part of my mind has been chewing on ideas for days, even years, then the synthesis appears. The great joy in the process of writing itself is the seemingly endless number of surprises that appear.

I sometimes create an outline, well, not so much an outline as a rapidly scribbled task list. Thought patterns of how I will get from the beginning to the end. I wrote such a list for my first book. In about an hour, on two sheets of my notepad, I jotted down headings that became chapters. With that list hanging on a hook just outside my peripheral vision, I started at the top and wrote for six months. By the time my editor had finished her work, the final product only varied from that original list in small ways. Chapter titles had changed and some original ideas where tossed in the editing process, but I can still look at those two pages and see the book.

I am writing all the time in my subconscious until pieces ooze out into my conscious world. Sometimes, sitting in my overstuffed, comfy chair reading, my dog curled in my lap, I realize that I have locked onto a word in a book, a trigger of sorts, and stopped moving my eyes forward on the page. Suddenly, I am creating a fully formed paragraph for something completely different. I see the text and edit it as if the words are floating in the air all around me. I change a word, insert a new sentence and read it back to myself, hear it in my own voice. When I am satisfied, I drop back into the reality of the book in my hand and keep reading. Rarely will I hunt for pen and paper or the Notepad app on my phone and jot down what I have created. Part of me is annoyed I couldn't stay focused on what I was reading. I can't decide if I am being lazy or have come to trust that whatever appeared will remain there somewhere until I need it. When I do take the time to jot down the musings and return to my note the next day, I most often think it is junk and just write.

It doesn't take much distance from the original composition for my amnesia to kick in, but years later, the effect is startling. When I was writing my memoir, I opened boxes of papers I had written forty years ago. I vaguely recognized certain stylistic fingerprints, some which remain with me today, but all those words … where did they come from? Some of the writing was wonderful, little rhetorical twists and turns of phrase. Some was clearly the effort of an inexperienced young man. There is no shortage of incoherent awfulness. Page after page, I wonder why I don't recognize myself.

The effect is stranger still for what I wrote as a later-in-life graduate student about a decade ago. The writing then was tightly reined in by the demands of academia. I marvel at detailed arguments I have no memory of making. When I wrote and bound my 100-page master's thesis, I sent a copy to my parents. A proud moment for me, my mom said she wanted a copy. Before her descent into Alzheimer's, she made a little shrine. In a rack, dusted once a week, a copy of the thesis remains in its honored place on a shelf. Mom is gone now, but on a visit, I was sitting at the dining room table with Dad, a voracious reader, and pointed at my black bound thesis.

"You ever read that one?"

"I tried," he said, shaking his head. "That one isn't much fun. I could never keep going on it."

Truth is, when I picked it up again and thumbed through it, neither could I. Who wrote that?

There are a handful of sections in my memoir that were very hard to write. Dogs, baseball, and my wife mostly. I remember the effort it took to keep the keyboard clicking like a court recorder as I cried and sniffed and took deep breaths. As the words poured out of me, the past was alive, smelling the wet fur of my long-departed dogs, feeling the sun on my face at a game, or the pressure of Sally's arms around me, her hands on my back. These were life events that marked me, stories that had become part of my personal iconography. Then, as part of the writing process … I rewrote them … a dozen times, sometimes more. I buffed and polished them until those words shined. I read them over again as proof copies of the book reached my desk.

Then, months removed, a friend asked me a question about a passage from the book. I had to search through the pages until I could find the page that would answer her question. I couldn't remember what I had said. Once I began reading, I couldn't put the book down. There I was on the page, but the writing seemed new. I got to one of the stories that I had cried through in the writing. A few paragraphs in, I was in tears again, and when I reached the emotional apex of the story I was heaving in a familiar emotional release. The story was part of me, but my amnesia had kicked in and suddenly the telling was all new.

There are some things that should remain a mystery. There was a time when people possessed of gifts seen as strange, or even miraculous, were forced from the clan to live in hovels or caves on the outskirts of the village. Their gifts were unnatural and frightened others. A curious few would make pilgrimages to consult the hermits, to touch that thing that scared them. My amnesia, that alienation from the source, is like having a hermit living in my mind. I visit him and he brings out small gifts, little insights, small bites to savor. The rule is that each trip, each visit, is different. No well-used map will get me there every time. Maybe that is how it has to be. Maybe the true gift that little fellow gives me is the surprise I feel whenever I come back to what I have created. I don't know, but for now that will have to do.

HAIRCUT

EARLY MARCH, in the year of COVID-19, days from Oregon going into the quarantine, my hair was getting shaggy, so I scheduled a haircut. Never in my life have I spent so much time thinking about a simple haircut. Well … when I was in the throes panic disorder, I dreaded haircuts because for fifteen minutes I could not escape the barber's chair. But this was new and different. I thought of the chair and the people rotating through it. I thought about how many times my barber touches people day after day, week after week. I thought about if I would shake his hand coming and going. Mostly, I thought, is this safe or a completely dumb idea?

My longtime barber and all his peers look like a 1950s Rock-a-Billy band. In fact, many of them are in those kinds of bands. Psycho-Billy. Punk-a-Billy. All the Billys. Lots of tattoos starting at their necks, and neatly cut, slicked back hair. Chains dropped from wallets. Rolled cuff Levi's 501 jeans, never washed, just left to wear in and form fit to their bodies. Biker boots. Nice collection of old-school Harleys neatly parked on the street outside. Not choppers, retro softail cruisers. The crew is always friendly, but it sometimes feels like an inside joke is floating around the room. The Rock-a-Billy station is streaming all the time with barbers occasionally making remarks on the songs. I like the place. We talk cars and punk rock. I have gone out to see my barber and his band at shows. I suppose I get a little credibility as the old dude who is always telling them what punk shows I've seen lately. And it's hard to slide any car reference by me.

Thinking about the haircut, I have never been so conscious that I am sixty-four-years-old. Because I was tracking the coronavirus from the time it appeared in China, I had basically gone into isolation early on. Now COVID-19 had me hyper-conscious that I am in the 'greatest risk' cohort. Here I thought that age would mostly be about wisdom, free time, and discounts at a movie. Silly me.

I decided to go ahead and get the haircut, a little shorter than usual, Army tight on the sides, so I would not need another one so soon. In the door, as usual, my guy offered me a beer or a shot of whiskey (yeah, it's that kind of place) and his hand. I froze, stepped back, and looked him in the eye. Not sharing a firm handshake with these men and women is an insult.

I said, "Good to see you, man. You know, I'm over sixty, kind of the danger zone for this virus thing, so for the duration I am not shaking hands. Okay?"

Ray held his hand out in the air, then dropped it as a serious look crossed his face. "Yeah, man, I get that."

The folks there talked about the hysteria surrounding the approaching virus and the craziness of hoarding hand sanitizer, paper towels, and toilet paper.

Ray said, "I use a lot of bleach wipes and can't find any."

I was being careful. I didn't want to get political, but I had been deep diving into virus news for weeks and wanted to impart some of what I learned. I felt something new about these guys and gals. I wanted them to be safe. I cared that they survived. These are the kind of folks who by nature offer a little more respect to their elders. When I retired, Ray made a nod toward my new status by dropping his fee to the retired guy price. I upped his tip to cover the new difference.

I told the crew that I mostly blew off the cable news and went looking for scientists and epidemiologists. I got them up-to-date on what was happening in the early virus wave to the north in Seattle. I tried to restrain my natural inclination to being pedantic. I knew they would tune out if I did that. I mixed it up. We talked about rock shows that wouldn't happen and basketball being played in empty arenas. Now on the same page, I told them the stories of the doctors in Italy. Brutal, life and death triage and not enough hospital beds. Then one of the toughest looking characters in the bunch, a generally quiet one, said in a low voice, "Yeah, I am not sure what to do with my kid if schools shut down."

There was genuine worry in his voice. I guess I had made the mistake of assuming they were lone wolves. Kind of a dumb assumption, mostly my weird fantasy. My city, hell my block, is full of fully tattooed men and women pushing baby strollers. It was a little startling the first time I saw that, but I quickly recalibrated. Of course, he had a child. And of course, given what was coming, that was his first thought.

Early on in the crisis, time compressed, events snowballed. By time I got home that day, in the short time I was in the barber's chair, the NCAA announced that March Madness would not have crowds. WHO declared an official pandemic. The stock markets dropped into a bear market. My San Francisco Giants killed the bay series with Oakland. Seattle closed all schools. And the president was once again on television trying to wish it all away.

Ray finished the cut. Standing up, I said, half-joking, "You guys do know that all you are going to have to shave your beards to wear masks, right?"

"What?" said Ray.

"I heard that," said the tough guy, "the whiskers collect the virus."

"Maybe put a sign in the window offering to shave the hipsters at a discount," I said as everyone laughed.

"Wash those hands, stay safe," I said as I put on my coat to leave.

When I got back to my car, I cleaned my hands with sanitizer, then went home to do the rest of my coronavirus haircut plan. I took off all my clothes and put them in the wash. Then I took a long, hot shower. Out of the shower, there was more news from Italy. The prime minister had closed all shops but pharmacies and food marts. Barbershops, too? I wondered.

I knew the privilege of being Americans would not let us escape this virus. It was coming hard and fast. During those early days, in spite of the warnings, Americans remained mostly clueless. That day, I listened to right wing radio on the drive home. The talker was calling it the Wuhan Flu. Nice propaganda, I thought; make it foreign and like the flu. Except, testifying before Congress that morning, one of those CDC doctors we soon would all know too well said that the absolute best case is that the mortality of COVID-19 will be ten times that of the flu. Death estimates exceeded understanding. Just numbers so large they would not register.

So, I got a haircut. Home, seemingly safe again, I was still thinking about the future of my buddies at the punk rock barbershop. How will they make a living, pay the rent and care for their kids when the virus cloud now enveloping Seattle shifted south? I didn't know.

106 days later, I knew. Because it was down the street from me, I had walked past the empty barbershop dozens of times in the quiet of the lock down. I stopped to look at the sign on the glass door, noticed my masked reflection, and wondered how the barbers were doing.

During the lock down, I created a little lonely project to get out of the house. In an old picture from the 1918 flu pandemic I had seen a hand-lettered closed sign in a shop. It occurred to me that there must be hundreds of those around the city now and they would disappear as soon as we reopened. Mask on, I took long walks of all the business districts, camera in hand, shooting pictures of every sign I could find. I got a little exercise and felt like a strange historian of over 500 signs of frozen commerce. Every sign was sad in its own way, but the long, handwritten, hopeful ones were the worst. Some had assumed they would be back soon. It was not to be. In the long avenues of closed shops, empty bars and restaurants struggling to get by on to-go orders, my little barbershop struck a special chord. I had no way to reach Ray. I knew he lived nearby, group house, I thought.

Sitting in his chair over the years, I had heard about his

happy motorcycle trips and how he didn't have enough money to get his car fixed properly so he did a workaround to keep it going. Once he confided that maybe he needed to lay off the booze for a while because he wasn't doing anything good with his time. I encouraged him to write some more songs and tell me where I could see him play. But like so many of the barbers, waiters, bakers, and bartenders on the street, I knew that now he had to be barely hanging on. Ray was the face I most readily saw when I heard the stories about small businesses closing and delayed unemployment checks.

For a while, I liked how my hair was growing out. My call to cut the sides extra short was prescient. I was looking better than some of my friends—well, the ones with hair— not those who only needed to run razer to tidy up their noggin. Then my hats didn't fit so well. The long hair made the thin parts on top look thinner and the sides took on a Bozo-like protrusion. When the weather heated up, the hair over my collar really bugged me. I tried to think of the last time my hair was so long. I think it was in the early 80s when I briefly lived like a fake hippie in the green mountains of eastern Washington. Well, there was also an unfortunate period where I sported a momentarily fashionable short ponytail and single small gold hoop earring. Let's not linger with that image.

My county, the most population dense in the state, was the last to reopen. Barbers would be among the early freed. Stroking my scraggly locks as I read at night, I began to consider what it would be like to get a haircut. But now I knew more, and the new calculation included a startling thought, "Would I die for a haircut?" *What?* I had heard the stories of stubbornly resistant barbers who had kept their shops open and then died of COVID-19. This was a serious business, this cut and a trim. I took solace in one curious story of a legally open shop where two of the hair stylists had tested positive for the virus and the authorities had contact traced over 150 customers. Less miracle and more science, none of the customers had caught the disease. Masks had saved the day. I wrapped myself around that story and waited for my barbershop to be open for a couple of weeks. This was not a time to be an early adopter and two weeks was enough to see if anyone else came down with COVID-19 at my shop. Yeah, let someone else be the test case. Good Lord, how mercenary a pandemic can make one.

I made the appointment. On the day before, I got a text from Ray. That had never happened before. Merely seeing his sentence on my phone made me happy. He warned that I would only get in the shop when he was ready, masks were mandatory, and he was not taking credit cards—cash or Venmo only so I didn't have to touch his phone. I liked all those precautions. There are new things we can take seriously to save lives. They are simple acts related to shared consequences, a new layer of complexity to humanity in a pandemic. Ray, it seemed, was on my team.

In the 106 days my hair grew, I had thought a lot about my first haircut. Time to think and strange things to consider. Raised a blue-collar kid, I have always retained an immense respect for people who work with their hands, whose skills never make them rich but whose lives are rich nonetheless. I was a little worried about Ray. My wife had been paying her hair stylist for non-haircuts for the duration. I had no way to do that with Ray. Instead, I mentally ran his tab hoping for the day I could pay him for all those missed haircuts.

When I arrived, there was a new bench in front of the

shop. The barber without a customer was now a guard of sorts. I gave him my name and he said to wait outside. He called in the cracked open door and through the glass I could see Ray acknowledge I was waiting. He was cleaning the chair. All good signs.

Ray donned a blue bandana, very on brand. I wished he had a surgical mask like me but he had a huge beard now. We assumed our safe bubbles as I approached the chair. Now, in the new world, interpersonal communication is all about the eyes and mask muted voices. Optimistically, maybe foolishly, I asked Ray for my usual and not the short tight cut of months ago.

We began our usual chat. Maybe not so usual. He talked about how his hair had gone wild during the shutdown. I told him my how my hair was now officially driving me nuts. Conscious that he was telling his quarantine story to customer after customer, after letting him know he and his coworkers had been much in my thoughts, I turned to a serious matter.

"Have you gotten your unemployment checks?"

"No," he said, "I keep checking and there is nothing. One of my buddies finally got all of his back checks at once."

I told him I was furious about how the state had failed people.

"That is so fucked up. Man, what about your rent? Is your landlord being cool?

As I said it, I thought I had gone too far. Ray has always appeared to be a proud man and I pursed my lips under my mask.

"No, he's been very cool. My housemate is working, and the landlord knows we are good for it when this all turns. In fact, he came by with a box of food and stuff for us."

There it was. That thing humans do when you start to lose hope for the entire species. Understanding and kindness against self-interest.

"What a great guy," I responded.

There was new haircut ballet to do. An ear at a time I pulled the elastic bands of my mask off one side, then the other, keeping the mask over my face with my free hand. As we talked, I realized how starved I had been for a simple conversation with another soul. COVID-19 had curated my contacts to people I knew well. In the one grocery store where I feel safe all transactions take place through a plexiglass barrier. Talking to Ray, I realized how much I treasure my little interactions with strangers. Each contact is an opportunity to gather intel from the human race. I love the tangents that appear when two people briefly find a connection, a shared passion or gentle disagreement. I began to fear that I was jabbering on too much with Ray, almost unconscious of the haircut itself, and then he was done.

I had long ago decided what I would pay for this first haircut. On the way to the shop, I had driven by an ATM and taken out five crisp twenty dollar bills.

Ray stood next to the chair.

"So, you have my phone number now," he said. "If this all goes to hell, I went out and found an antique barber's chair and put it in my garage. Just text me and we can set something up. Your usual … $25."

Obsessively anticipating the moment, I purposely wore a shirt with a front pocket and reached into it pulled out the folded bills and handed them to him.

"I figure I have missed a few haircuts and want to help you get back on your feet."

"Wow, Jim. Thanks. I really appreciate it."

"Look, one day this will be over. You and I are going to run into each other at a show. Buy me a shot of whiskey when we meet."

"You got it," he said as I walked out.

Now the routine, all planned. Hands sanitized. Straight up to the bathroom. Stripped down, clothes abandoned and a hot shower. The hot water felt good through my short hair.

The haircut didn't end with the shower. I had a counter going in my head … days since the haircut exposure. Three days after, I had an unhappy gut all day. I was anxious. This is a COVID-19 symptom. A well-trained hypochondriac, I kept checking my temperature and waiting for a dry cough. Crazy making. When I told my wife about my gut, I was cross with her because she didn't take me serious enough, but then she gave me her well-practiced, 'oh honey' look.

Then she said, "It's all the ice cream."

As a treat, she had brought home a gallon of mint chip. I couldn't get enough of it. We almost never buy ice cream, let alone a gallon. My stomach wasn't happy about all that sugar and fat. So much for my virus crisis.

Weeks have passed. My hair is getting longer. I look at the calendar on my office wall and wonder when I will schedule the next haircut. Mostly, I think about what it will be like once again not to care.

ACKNOWLEDGMENTS

THE MURDEROUS LITTLE VIRUS demanded an all-encompassing distraction. While I won't thank COVID-19, this second book may not have had the same urgency in a saner time.

I am once again grateful for the patience and passion of Hannah Kuhn. She took the time to aim her considerable love of the written word at my early manuscript and gave me both incisive criticism and steadfast encouragement. That is a rare skill.

A few of the essays herein had their genesis as slivers of what they became on my fast and dirty essay website www.noclock.org. The comments and critiques from readers both challenged and encouraged me to make those early experiments whole.

My editor, Jami Carpenter, saw what I could no longer see and made the text immeasurably better.

As always, I am grateful for the patience and support of family and friends who smile knowingly as I chatter on about my latest writing discoveries.

Sally Blackwood, my wife and lockdown partner, is the grace in my life that allows me to indulge this writing obsession. Let's meet at break time in the kitchen for coffee.

Finally, our dogs. Mozy, the suddenly blind girl, reminds us that adaptation is glorious. And my little boy dog, Zoom, who evidently can tell time as he demands a break from me to throw the Frisbee every day at 3 PM. He keeps us both sane.

ABOUT THE AUTHOR

———————————————

JIM BLACKWOOD, JR. grew up in the Southern California desert and lived on both sides of the country before settling in Portland, Oregon. He caught the politics and public service bug early and worked on a Senate staff in Washington DC before becoming a successful information systems manager for two decades. Hearing the call of his first love, he switched careers to become a senior policy director for a Portland city commissioner.

In 2017, Jim became a fulltime writer and in 2019 published his memoir *Am I Cured Yet? My Wonderful Life with Panic Disorder and PTSD*. He writes essays for his website www.noclock.org and is a contributor to the digital health community TheMighty.com.

Jim has a Master of Arts in Interdisciplinary Studies focused on political science and religion. He is a student of Zen Buddhism and baseball, which he feels are pretty much the same thing. When not living the COVID-19 lockdown lifestyle, he can be found at local rock clubs, at his favorite

100-year-old movie theater, or in his third-row seats watching the Portland Pickles baseball team. For now, you can find him scooting his GTI around Oregon countryside roads or tending his dahlia garden which has never looked better. As Jim's grandmother used to say, "Lord willing and the creek don't rise" he hopes to find himself in a major league ballpark as soon as the virus allows.

Jim and his wife of 23 years, Sally, live high atop Mt. Tabor with their dogs Zoom and Mozy.

~

To contact Jim, learn about future projects, purchase his books or read his blog, please visit:
www.jimblackwoodjr.com.

www.ingramcontent.com/pod-product-compliance
Lightning Source LLC
Chambersburg PA
CBHW070823120626
46556CB00002B/637